New Year

Cows in the Corn

By the same author:

'Milk my Ewes and Weep'

Cows in the Corn

JOYCE FUSSEY

With best wishes,
Joyce Fussey

Paul Elek   London

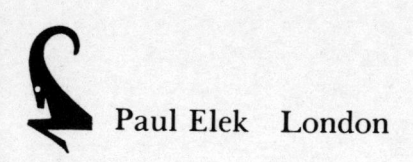

For Miss Margaret H. Mair

Published in Great Britain 1978 by
Paul Elek Ltd.
54-58 Caledonian Road, London N1 9RN

Copyright © Joyce Fussey 1978

All rights reserved. No part of this publication
may be reproduced, stored in a retrieval system
or transmitted, in any form or by any means,
electronic, mechanical, photocopying, recording
or otherwise, without the prior permission of
the publishers.

ISBN 0 236 40149 1

Printed in Great Britain by
Billing Limited, Guildford, Surrey

Contents

1	Trespassers	7
2	Four wheels and a board	12
3	Belle Starr rides again	16
4	Will Perseus please come forward?	20
5	Overture to winter	25
6	Mush! Mush!	30
7	A winter's tale	39
8	Spring's awakening	44
9	Lofty ambitions	49
10	It keeps us off the streets	55
11	Emergency ward	63
12	Enter Charlotte	68
13	Friends in need	72
14	Mellow fruitlessness	77
15	Tree talk	82
16	Stonecrop	86
17	A mad whirl in town	89
18	MRCVS	95
19	Tip	99
20	A fowl tale	105
21	Sheep may safely graze	109
22	'Lhude sing cuccu'	113
23	*Haec olim meminisse juvabit*	117
24	Tails you win	121
25	Heads we lose	129
26	The builders are coming	134
27	Home and dry	139

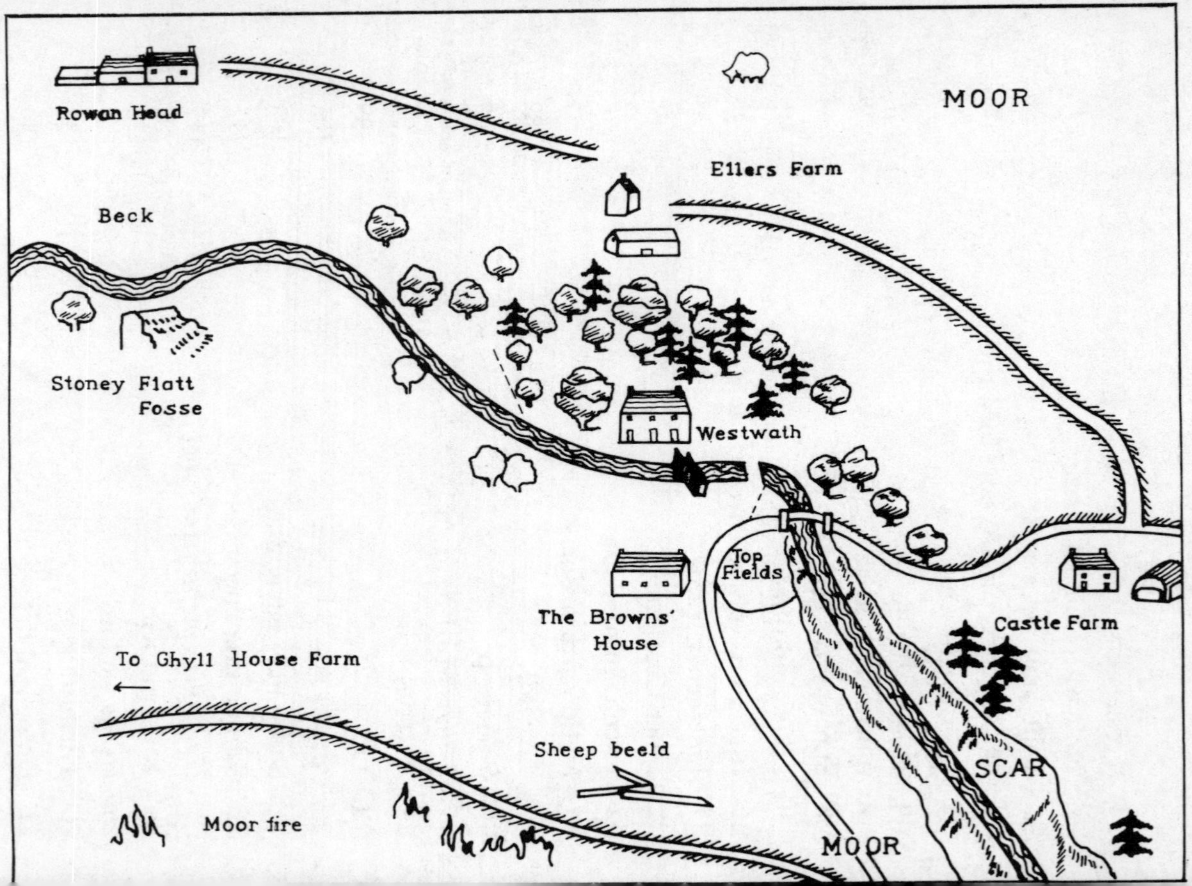
Rowan Head
MOOR
Ellers Farm
Beck
Stoney Flatt
Fosse
Westwath
Top
Fields
The Browns'
House
Castle Farm
To Ghyll House Farm
Sheep beeld
SCAR
Moor fire
MOOR

1 Trespassers

When you consider the ease and regularity with which situations tend to flare up at Westwath it is not surprising that my husband takes my personal conflagrations in his stride.

'Your thumb's on fire again,' he said one day when we had lived a year and a half at Westwath. And very helpfully he turned on the cold water tap for me.

In a hissing cloud of steam I extinguished the blaze and pulled off another soggy bandage. Obligingly Gordon passed me a new one. Did I know, he said wonderingly, that we had gone through another packetful?

I wasn't surprised. We wear bandages as other people wear clothes, and I turned myself into a human torch every time I struck a match to light the gas lamp.

New-fangled electricity hadn't yet caught on here at our smallholding in a wooded oasis in the fastness of the North Yorkshire Moors and we used Calor gas for lighting, cooking and ironing. There was also a gas fire which we fetched out of the holiday bungalow after the last weekly tenants had departed, and there were oil lamps for groping our way to bed, so I had unlimited opportunity for setting fire to my bandages. This time my thumb was swaddled in a beauty. It looked like a wasps' nest on a stick. It was cosseting a swollen, purple digit — the outcome of an uneven contest with a blackthorn bush which was better armed than I was. Part of the needle-like spine was still in there somewhere under a poultice of glycerine, Epsom salts and throbbing flesh. Going gangrenous, I shouldn't wonder.

It was all the fault of Joe Stewart's Dad's red Hereford heifer.

Some of the Stewarts' land lies on the far side of the beck facing our long, narrow calf field and garden, and abutting the hummocky, scrubby pasture we call the garage field (because we garage the car on its farther side by the road) at the boundary fence by the footbridge. This neighbouring land is steep, undulating and wooded; consequently very attractive to trespassers who drive the Stewarts — and us — mad when they break through the fence in order to follow the beck to Stoney Flatt Foss, a waterfall which sings or roars over tabular rocks according to the mood of the beck at the time. It is more easily accessible from the path across the moor but the majority of the map-reading public ignore that and choose to shred their clothes on Joe's barbed wire in the traditional masochistic way of the holidaying British.

Over the years we have been amazed how few people can read a map. Dozens of ramblers hung about with cameras, binoculars and sheaves of maps and local guides have stood, heavy-booted, on my capitulating lavender hedge, looking vacantly about them for the waterfall which, by their reckoning, ought to be cascading down our front steps. One couple told me categorically that High Ellers Foss was slap bang behind our vegetable garden. So numerous are the lost souls knocking at our door that all strangers hesitating at the garden gate are presumed to be Stoney Flatt Fossils before ever they open their mouths. But no one should be so disorientated as to do what one family did — march across our neighbours' garden and up the steps to the side entrance, treck through the breakfast room to the dining-room where the Browns innocently sat at tea, and, without any preliminaries, demand to be directed to the waterfall. With enviable presence of mind Binnie replied, 'Up the stairs, across the landing and straight on through the front bedroom'!

Because of all these unauthorised entrances our fences were not what they had been; sometimes the Stewarts' stirks accidentally fell through when they were leaning over bawling pleasantries at our cows, and sometimes they broke through on purpose when they felt the call of love and got carried away by emotion. The red Hereford heifer was particularly prone to this and would get in amongst our cows where she formed an unnatural attachment to Rhoda whom she mistook for a bull because of the horns. She always did it after Gordon had set off for work and the boys to school. I could never get her back on my own and would have to phone Joe who would come with unhurried gait and a couple of dogs, and with a few meaningful whistles and a 'Gerowertheer' or two, send the frustrated animal splashing back to her own side of the stream.

After one such incident it rained hard all night and as I crossed the footbridge the beck was flowing fast and deep. The heifer was still serenading Rhoda at the top of her lungs and I jeered at her as I passed. 'Yah, boo,' I said. 'That'll fettle you,' I said. 'Can't get across that lot,' I said, and went blithely on my way to the village and caught the bus to the local town. The river was even higher, I noted, when I returned. There was no sign of the heifer as I mounted the bridge steps, which wasn't surprising as she was over in our calf field playing ring o' roses with Rhoda, Bluebell and Rosie. If Leander could do it so could she.

With an anguished screech I broke a stick from a convenient bush and waded into the mêlée whacking resolutely at the heifer's rump but, as is always the case when I seize a stick in an emergency, it was a long, thin, brittle thing which snapped off a section at each wallop until I was left with a six-inch bit only suitable for a tent peg. But reinforcements were arriving. Robert and Antony had returned from school accompanied by Pauline, their great friend and engineering partner from Castle Farm 'next door'. Between all of us we held the heifer at bay and chivvied our three into the next field where they ought to have been in the first place. Robert swiftly fastened the gate behind the cows and, overcome with excitement, they galloped the length of the meadow like steeplechasers, the red heifer keeping pace parallel but four feet below because the calf field is that much lower than its neighbour.

By this time, Jess, our erstwhile sheepdog, had entered the

arena and with her help we chased our lot into the *next* field, the back one behind the bungalow, and Robert shut that gate too. It was in the nick of time because the heifer — steeplechasing having gone to her head — had wheeled about, taken a run and was clearing the wall which tops the bank as if she was taking Becher's — if I hadn't seen it with my own eyes I wouldn't have believed it. She seemed a bit surprised herself, and for a few seconds trotted about the hayfield collecting her wits and bearings then, egged on by shouts from the other cows, she made a bee-line towards us until brought up by the thorn and barbed wire fence.

'Into the cowhouse with'em, lads,' I cried, as the three cows lined up to bellow encouragement, but before we were half-way to the farmyard gate the heifer performed a further show-stopping feat (she was wasted on a farm — as a stunt cow she would have been a wow). Turning her back but casting a measuring glance over her shoulder to make sure she was on target, she swung her bottom round and vigorously rammed the fence with it. A post snapped in two like a runner bean. With a creak, another sank to the ground. The wire sagged, and following up on her advantage the bovine battering ram drove in stern first and was joyfully greeted and fêted by her friends.

'Now what?' asked the children of their leader.

I considered deeply. 'We'll go and have tea,' I said.

Unfortunately, after tea things were very much the same except that the evening had become much darker. The girls were busily socialising and told us, flatly, that they were *not* coming in for milking and what did we intend to do about it? What I did was phone the Stewarts.

Some time and many degrees of darkness later, a torchlight wavering up the yard warned me that Joe had arrived. I went to meet him with a lighted hurricane lamp.

'Noo then, Joyce,' said Joe in greeting.

'Hello, Joe,' I returned and poured out the tale of his heifer's daring exploits.

'Why, I deeant reckon she'll gan far,' said Joe placidly. 'Let's have a go at getting 'em in.'

Actually it was no trouble at all getting them in. All of them.

The heifer came too and squeezed in line between Rosie and her dear friend, Rhoda. Nice place they had here, she observed. Not a lot of room though.

The heifer rested her chin affectionately on Rhoda's shoulder and wriggled comfortably, but Rhoda, delighted though she was to entertain company outside in the pasture, thought it overstepping the mark when that same company looked dangerously likely to be sharing her bucket of dairy nuts. She jumped resentfully back into the dung channel just as Rosie swung round to march outside again.

For a few minutes it was checkmate with the cowhouse a solid jam of bodies and me wondering what the next move ought to be. Bluebell, at least, was out of it. She was standing well forward in her stall, head in bucket, keeping her cool and unshakably gathering a couple of pounds of cownuts into safe keeping.

Rosie having flounced out into the yard, there was more room for the rest of us and Joe came in to deal with the gate-crasher. She was going anyway, she sniffed with a last regretful look at Rhoda who had turned her back and was ostentatiously eating her nuts. She wouldn't stay where she wasn't wanted, and she swung sharply about, colliding in the doorway with Rosie — who had just remembered that she hadn't had her tea and was on her way back to attend to it.

Somehow Joe got both animals outside and I fastened Rhoda's chain just as she brought her head up to glare round at the disturbance from which she now utterly dissociated herself. But I had been caught like that once before and was standing well back so her horns hardly damaged me at all. Then, urged on by Joe, Rosie drove in like an express train and buried her head in her bucket, grunting, the while, her disapproval of the whole affair. I slipped outside and hurriedly snecked the door.

Of the heifer there was no sign; she had made off in the dark in the direction of the muckheap all set, judging by her speed when last seen, to jump over the moon ...

Next day Joe and his dad came across to see where she had got in this time. She had come home as if nothing had happened, Joe reported! There was no fence at their side of the beck and she had broken through ours into the vegetable garden in just about the spot where High Ellers Foss would have been if those ramblers had been right.

Mr Stewart and Joe repaired the fence with posts and barbed wire and, for good measure, I rammed in a blackthorn bush which had recently been uprooted by the Waterboard men when they were laying a pipe close by.

A needle-like spine ran into my thumb and broke off ...

2 Four wheels and a board

During the equivalent of a lifetime since we had swapped the nerve-racking cares of city dwelling for the mind-bending anxieties of country life, we had learned many things. Among them —
1. Cows are cleverer than we are.
2. Sheep are cleverer than anybody — even cows.
3. Sheep will —. Sheep can —. Well, sheep are capable of absolutely anything at all which is the reason we had recently sold all ours.
4. Eggs should never be carried in jacket pockets.

Another thing we had learned was that there were far more autumn leaves in the country than in town. Round, diamond-shaped, lance-shaped, palm-shaped, arrow-shaped and just plain leaf-shaped they fluttered from trees in their millions and stopped up the house gutters, fall pipes and sinks. They lay on the fields like Persian carpets and the cows came along like vacuum cleaners and sucked them up. They covered the surface of the beck until it resembled terraza flooring, stacked up in layers against the wath and choked up its pipes. They filled the lanes like snowdrifts and drove against the window panes with the rattle of hail. Like desert dunes they settled in heaps only to rise again in swirling eddies and re-form elsewhere. I was delighted. All that lovely nourishing leaf-mould for the garden.

'You'd wonder where they all came from', said my 76-year-old mother as she packed them into cattle-food bags for easier carrying to the compost heap. Knee deep in them, nineteen months old Roger helped her. He had been walking and talking since he was ten months old and we were glad to find something to occupy him, I can tell you. Everyone not actually suffering from rigor mortis is pressed into service here.

Straight from school Robert, Antony and Pauline could be seen diligently filling sacks and I would beam on them encouragingly and hand out winegums to reward their industry. At bedtime they would still be filling sacks so it was puzzling that the compost heap grew so slowly. Until I noticed that whereas mother and Roger trundled their sacks to the right, past the front of the house and away round to the heap, Pauline and the two boys lugged them to the left and down the yard.

'Hoy,' I called cheerfully, 'that's the wrong place. The compost heap is in the vegetable garden.'

The trio looked at me as if I wasn't right. 'Compost heap,' they said witheringly, 'these aren't for a *compost* heap. They're for our bonfire. We've got seventy-four bagsful of them.'

It was going to be a super fire, they said. They'd got an old three-piece suite as well, and *stacks* of wood and had I got an old coat for the guy? Why didn't I come up to Castle Farm and see it?

So the next Saturday I did, accompanied by my friend, Marjorie, who was staying with us for the weekend. We were respectfully impressed by the bonfire pile which was the size and shape of Vesuvius and looked potentially as dangerous.

Privately, Marjorie and I thought it would still be burning at Christmas and were thankful that it was in the middle of a five acre field and well away from anywhere — particularly Westwath.

Those kids never did anything by halves. Their 'lorry' was

a case in point. I suppose most children make bogies and soap-box cars but the contrast between our lorry and a bogie was as great as that between a spaceship and a wheelbarrow.

Robert and Pauline, who was almost as mechanically minded as he was — and he was a natural, viewing the world through a film of oil and only registering matters connected with gaskets, sockets, spigots and stroboscopic ignition timing — had been working on this masterpiece of engineering for months in every available minute. It was as long as a United bus and almost as heavy, as Marjorie and I saw when, bursting with pride, the two 10-year-olds introduced us to it. Patently, every farm dump in the area had been plundered for components. Apparently there was a rich seam of disintegrating vehicles at Rowan Head and the children had been going up there regularly — usually on Fridays which, by a remarkable coincidence, was Mrs Hewson's baking day — and walking the mile long lane back to Castle Farm humping unwieldy objects with attractive possibilities.

(One day the haul included a very tiny kitten which they couldn't possibly leave up there to starve, because it hadn't a home. Mrs Hewson said it wasn't one of theirs. She didn't know where it had come from and it would probably die. They couldn't leave it to *starve*, could they, so what else could they do? And we hadn't a cat now and they couldn't leave it to —

'But Robert,' I said, doubting Mrs Hewson's innocence but admiring her recourse, 'just where did you find it?'

I received a typically Robert-like reply. 'On the front off side suspension,' he answered simply.)

Anyway, there loomed the lorry — blue, red, bitumen black and cumbrous — and Marjorie and I admired it greatly, from its lavishly oiled axles, its battery of horns, headlamps and gauges, to the unexpected embellishment of the dented AA badge fixed to the front bumper.

They would just put the wheels back on, said Pauline, then we could all have a ride.

Antony plus Pauline's two younger brothers added their strength to haul the juggernaut up the Rowan Head lane —

it had a good incline, a feature essential to a gravity powered lorry — and we all climbed aboard, five children, Marjorie, Pauline's mother, Joan Arrowsmith and me. There was only one padded seat — the driver's — which was allocated to me in deference to my advanced age but the others all found perches round about. Pauline and Robert shoved the thing off and clambered on. Robert pushed in beside me and seized the steering wheel, and the ponderous equipage moved off. We all clung to the sides as it gathered speed. Creaking, rattling and squealing it lurched over pebbles and potholes, heeling like a racing dinghy round the bend where the Arrowsmith's black and white cows watched phlegmatically over a briar-bound hedge (fleetingly I wondered what Rosie, Rhoda and Bluebell would have made of it and could just see them having hysterics and giving no milk for a week), and hurtling down the straight towards — my conscience! — the main road ahead.

'Stop, Robert. Stop!' I screamed — I must have been out of my mind to allow this to happen. 'Put the brake down, for goodness sake!'

Robert bent over the steering wheel with the confidence of a Stirling Moss. 'Oh, I can't,' he said coolly. 'We haven't put any on yet.'

The main road rushed nearer. I prepared for the end. All at once the lorry lost speed and stopped — as the children knew it would — when it met a sudden slight incline yards in from the end of the lane. Those of us who weren't shot off the back climbed stiffly down on to the road.

'Did you enjoy that, Mrs Fussey?' cried Pauline, never doubting for a moment that I had.

'It was — exciting,' I answered truthfully. But it was nearly a year before Marjorie came to stay with us again.

The bonfire, of course, was a roaring success although Gordon, Roger and I caught only the tail of it. Robert and Antony had rushed off the minute tea was over. Roger and I waited for Gordon to return from work — a car journey of more than thirty miles — and he was later than he had intended to be. We arrived at Castle Farm just as everyone else, bouncing about on tractor and trailer, was leaving the

15

fire, but the children welcomed the excuse to return with us. There was little remaining of that gargantuan pile, although the circle of red hot embers as big as a circus ring was more than sufficient to roast us and kindle the non-banging sort of fireworks favoured by people like Roger and me. But Roger hardly noticed them. To him the biggest attraction, surpassing all the sparklers and Chrysanthemum Showers, was the moon, a huge dinner plate hanging overhead, still out of reach even though he was sitting on Daddy's shoulder and six feet nearer to it. Now that *was* something. Why hadn't somebody told him about it before?

As a matter of fact we had discovered it only recently, ourselves.

3 Belle Starr rides again

Who, living in town, really notices the moon? With street lamps, neon signs, electric light blazing from windows, the moon isn't necessary. Except, perhaps, to the romantically inclined. Out here a mile away from the nearest village street light we are glad of it and miss it terribly when it isn't there. Even indoors a shaft of moonlight lights a room better than a torch with the inevitable flat battery. But we appreciate its beauty too, and can be found on many an occasion, standing in the whitewashed landscape staring against it fully as hard as Meg Merrilies.

Without the moon I am lost but Gordon has an uncanny instinct for finding his way in the dark. He can come home late from work, walk in an unerring line over the garage field towards the wath and cross it into the yard as if guided by radar. Let me attempt the same thing and I jar my spine in craters and tangle with fences which until then I didn't even know existed. Saved only by a sudden glimpse of phosphorescence, more times than enough I have teetered on the edge of the beck assuring small, slightly hysterical children that of *course* I know where we are, and of *course* we shan't have to wait until Daddy comes home, praying earnestly the while for a car's headlights to sweep by and save us from a night camped on the river bank.

It was on a moonless night that Rupert, a black and white Friesian bullock, jumped over the half door of his pen and escaped to the freedom of the back field. The first I knew about it was when I noticed a formless white something floating over the boggy patch at the far end. Having recently read an article on spiritualism, I thought it was ectoplasm and almost passed out on the spot. I still couldn't move when the thing started towards me emitting gentle snorts. It was only when, almost upon me, it picked up speed and I heard its hooves pounding that the penny dropped.

I wasn't all that relieved even then, because that field boasted five gates, and so far as I could remember, all of them were open.

It was a race then, who got to each gate first. I only managed to because Rupert, showing off how he could run faster than I could, overshot each time, trotting back to breathe gustily over my shoulder as I thrust home the hooks. I was practically on my knees by the time I had circuited the field and secured all but the one leading into the yard by the hayshed through which, I hoped, he would return home. I really thought I had won when he made straight for it like a rocket and was already sighing with relief when, right on the blinking threshold, he pulled up so suddenly that his back legs overtook the front ones and he sat on his bottom with a thud that shook the ground.

Done it on purpose, he pretended, struggling to his feet and affecting an intense interest in the grassless, rutted mud between the gateposts to cover his embarrassment. Carefully I approached him, willing him to walk on through. Just as carefully he moved along the opening sniffing the ground as if it were old brandy until I was right on his tail when, with a whoop of derision, he swung about and zoomed past me into the darkness. I suddenly recalled that although the gates were now closed there was still an escapeway into the hayfield through the hole made by Joe's heifer.

I ran to the house for Jess who was delighted to come until she saw what was expected of her. For Jess didn't like stirks. With sheep she was in her element, a treat to watch; with the greatest of pleasure and efficiency she would round up the cows and bring them in at milking time; for driving hens out of the garden she was invaluable. But show her a stirk and she would promptly remember a bone she had buried a long way off which, if not attended to immediately, would be overdone. Why this was so we never discovered. We could only surmise that she had been kicked by a beast before we knew her; in her early days before she came to us with the farm.

'Get on, Jess,' I cried. 'Fetch him out.'

Instinctively obeying the order Jess shot into the field, realised what was in there and without bothering to change down turned round and came hurtling back like a boomerang, flattening herself in a corner by the hayshed and trying to look like a molehill. Only the tell-tale white patches on her long coat gave her away.

'Get *on*, Jess,' I shouted. 'GET ON.' And obviously she did because I saw her no more until all the excitement was over.

'If tha wants owt doing, tha'd best do it thisen' is a good old Yorkshire maxim which welcomed us from a plaque on the wall when we first moved into Westwath, and by gum, it is a truth we have lived with ever since. Tonight obviously was going to be no exception.

Blind Man's Buff in a drawing room is one thing, but played in an area of about an acre with an opponent possessing twice as many legs as oneself and not half using them, is another. Even though I had a long stick held out wide in each hand it left an awful lot of field for him to dodge about in.

Rupert was in his glory. How's that for a rodeo? He panted, practically standing on his head with excitement, heels kicking the sky as he passed me on his way downfield. Or this, he yelled jumping stiff-legged off all four feet at once on his way back. I puffed after him alternately whistling hopefully for Jess and swearing in what I thought was her general direction. She, needless to say, didn't appear but at every whistle Rupert came tearing up out of the dark to ask what I wanted and when I thwacked the ground under his nose with the sticks to check him, pieces flew off in all directions and I was left with the usual tent pegs.

I hardly ever swore before coming to Westwath, but I was learning fast.

Our holding lies in the valley ringed about by Castle, Ellers, Rowan Head and Ghyll House farms, and the house belonging to our nearest neighbours, Binnie and Steven Brown. It is an amphitheatre with those, our neighbours, in the gallery seats and we, half a mile or so below, occupying the arena. In summertime we are decently screened by a canopy of trees, and all but Rowan Head, which perches on the shoulder of a hill with only the sky for background like an illustration in a nursey rhyme book, is hidden from us. From sight, that is. Not out of earshot.

In the early part of our transition from town to country the sound of a tractor had me raking with binoculars those fields which were visible — not out of idle curiosity but because I thought that if *they* were doing something with tractors then we ought to be doing it too. Whatever it was. Mrs Hewson was also one for binoculars. Stuck up there like the farthest outpost of the Empire it kept her in touch and not much went on in our valley that she didn't know about.

In late winter, tractor noises accompanied by a rhythmical clanking means it is muck spreading time; in summer, a regular chunking tells us that they are baling already. There are also animal noises. At Ellers Farm the shrieking of geese reaches its peak just before Christmas and is significantly absent afterwards. A yipping of dogs keeps us informed of the postman's progress through Ellers farmyard and subsequent arrival at Rowan Head. A bulling heifer drives us mad for a couple of days with her monotonous insistent call and a babel of bleating tells us that it is sheep dipping time again. Familiar sounds with no close season include throbbing generators, growling chainsaws and rustic voices colourfully raised in expression of strong emotion.

I had no doubt that the Hewsons, Rawdons, Stewarts and Browns were at that very minute held spellbound by the sounds floating up from our back field. But I was past caring.

Five times had I got that blasted bullock to the yard gate and five times had he turned in its very mouth and pounded back to the marshy end, and there I was at the sixth attempt with him actually nosing past the gatepost when Robert appeared at the other side waving a hurricane lamp and asked, was I shouting?

Well how was he to know, he said reproachfully, going off to hang the lamp in a place of safety while I charged back into the fray once more.

This time, the two of us actually got Rupert into the yard, though before we could close the gate he had bolted through it again. That was the last straw. I marched back into the field and as Rupert bucked past once more I seized hold of his tail with every intention of swinging him around my head in the manner of Popeye and he was so surprised he ran straight through the yard and into his pen with me streaming behind like a kite.

Later that night when I went out to make sure everybody had quietened down, I found that Uncle Simon, another of the stirks, had been so carried away by the success of Rupert's adventure that he had let enthusiasm overrule commonsense (never his strong point), tried to break out through a space about six inches wide, and had got his head stuck fast.

All in all it was quite a night.

4   Will Perseus please come forward?

Robert doesn't take after me. I am not mechanically minded. At ten years of age Robert had taught himself to drive the car around our fields. At four times his age I hadn't even tried. I knew I couldn't do it. In a strange car I couldn't even open the door but sat winding the window up and down while whoever had given me a lift watched unbelievingly. I'm not really handy at all, to tell the truth, but there are things I just have to do. Drains to unstop, for instance, door hinges to replace, fences to secure, walls to build up, et cetera. On a good day I can hammer a nail half way in before it bends, but my best work by far is done with binder twine.

Not all the tangles of twine about the place at that time were mine — a number of repairs had already been carried out in this medium by the previous owner of Westwath — but the ones with the best knots were. (Knots being something I *am* good at — a craft learned in my Scouting days.) So, with an ever lengthening job list, Gordon was never without employment at weekends.

One Saturday in late November was a typical day.

Gordon had spent the morning scrambling along the edge of the beck through the rock strewn ravine searching for the roof ladders which had been swept away in a flood a short time previously, and having at length located them a mile away, he returned home for the car and went round by road to a more accessible point to collect them. In the afternoon he had planned to move some cattlefood, muck out a couple of calfpens, dig in new fenceposts to replace those demolished by the heifer, and to begin work on repairs to the ancient Fordson tractor.

The cattlefood was delivered by the agricultural suppliers to a hut by the gate at the top of our cart track and from there Gordon and the tractor would bring it down to be stored in bins in the doghouse. (That was where Jess spent her nights sorting sacks into untidy heaps. Every morning I shook out the sacks and folded them neatly on the raised padded bed I had made for her in a corner away from the draught, and every next morning she was found on the hard concrete floor surrounded by her dismantled bedding, utterly fagged out by the sleepless hours she had spent getting it like that.)

The tractor had been taken bad while transporting straw bales across the concrete ford (which here in North Yorkshire still goes by the old Norse name of wath) and was now laid up in the workshop awaiting a major operation, so

Gordon had to fetch the cattlefood in the Morris Traveller. He parked it on the wath while he cleared from the farmyard gateway a high ridge of sand deposited by the beck during its mad rampage at the time of the flood, and Jess, choosing that moment to have a brainstorm, tore across the footbridge and rounded up the cows for evening milking. At a quarter past two in the afternoon. It wouldn't have mattered had they been in any other field but the garage one, but to get into the yard from there they had to cross the wath — and the Traveller was taking up a good three-quarters of its width.

Rhoda and Rosie stopped in their tracks and carefully weighed up the situation, but Bluebell, hurrying up late, muttering that she was Boss-cow and ought to be in front and would have been if she hadn't been taken by surprise, shouldered them aside and attempted to pass the car. She hadn't a hope with that barrel of a tummy. It hit the car with a bonging sound and bounced off like a beachball clean over the edge of the wath.

It seemed ages before she hit the water. She hung as if suspended on strings, legs paddling vigorously like those push-along Mickey Mouses that children used to have, until gravity triumphed over even Bluebell's willpower and she entered the water with such an almighty splash that it parted like the Red Sea, exposing for one brief, startling moment the stony bed of the beck and creating a tidal wave which must have been felt in the next village.

Gordon and I were petrified.

Bluebell struggled to her feet, whipping up more high seas which broke along the banks and slapped against the wath. She would, of course, fall in at the deep side. At the other, it was only a matter of a couple of feet from the wath's surface to the riverbed — indeed the cows regularly paddled there — but where she stood then it was twice that depth and the riverbanks were more than double even that, and were steep, slippery and dangerously ribbed with tree roots to boot. The surface of the wath was level with her chest, without a foothold along its entire length. Certainly, with her figure, she couldn't jump up there. It was the bank or nothing. Gordon in his wellies, half wading half balancing on exposed rocks, hooshed her to the farther shore.

Bluebell all this time was very cross indeed. There stood Rhoda and Rosie still on the wath staring with pop-eyed excitement and enjoying every minute of it. Bluebell had never been so *humiliated*. Apart from that the water was icy, and if Gordon thought she was going to scale a cliff like the south face of the Matterhorn — she expecting her twelfth and all — he had another think coming. Swinging about, she splashed determinedly over to an island of shingle, turned her back on us and sulked.

'The only thing to do,' said Gordon, 'is to build a ramp.'

I was aghast. 'But it'll take ages. What about all the other jobs?'

'Can't be helped,' said Gordon. 'We'll build it in this corner. You could fetch those rocks from over there.'

Now phrases like that I hold entirely responsible for my remarkable structure. Biceps like an Irish navvy, says Gordon disparagingly. But it's not my fault. Years of tote that barge, lift that bale, have inevitably left their mark.

Gordon, wet to the elbows, was already prizing stones from the river-bed. They came up with a grating, sucking noise and water swirled in to take their place. He manhandled them to the corner where the wath met the rise into the farmyard and commenced building his ramp. Bluebell, still sulking, watched suspiciously from the corner of her eye.

Between us Gordon and I just about changed the course of the river and used up a good half hour of precious time. Any likelihood of work starting on the tractor that day, receded and vanished. Gordon packed another pebble or two in place and stepped back to admire his handiwork. 'There,' he said with satisfaction. 'We'll just get her out and then I'll go and start on that fence.'

We splashed over to Bluebell's island, turned her around and shoved her towards the slope. She shied away from it as if we were making her walk the plank and went back to her island feeling all of a flutter. She was a valuable cow, she would have us know, and we should have to do better than *that*. She burped up some cud and had a good chew to settle her nerves.

Mentally crossing the calfpens off our work list, Gordon and I set-to again, breaking our nails on chunks of rock which numbed our fingers and dripped water into our boots, staggering with them from yards away because we had cleared the immediate area of everything except shingle and megaliths.

Bluebell clung to her isle like Andromeda waiting for Perseus and we didn't half wish that he would materialise because she flatly refused to budge for us.

The afternoon wore on. We alternately added to the ramp and encouraged, incited, exhorted, coerced and goaded Andromeda to walk up it while she declined, resisted and refused point blank to do any such thing. At last, about teatime, when the ramp, packed tight with pebbles and sand, was as firm and smooth as a tarmac road and of a length that allowed a barely perceptible gradient and a width sufficient for a coach and four, we took a firm stand and a couple of sticks and set about her.

Bluebell shared a disgusted glare between the ramp and us, deliberately crossed in the opposite direction and went straight up the south face of the Matterhorn as if in a cliff-lift.

We got over it eventually, rubbed her down and gave her a warm bran mash. After all she was getting on a bit and was probably suffering from shock. After the bran she managed to take a bucket of dairy nuts and half a bale of hay which revived her so much that next morning, she made straight for the wath again and had to be firmly diverted to the back field.

At teatime on the following Saturday, while Gordon caught up on the fencing, I went to fetch in the cows from the top field. We crossed the deserted road and started to descend the steep cart-track which leads down to the wath, the cows, swinging heavy udders, walking in single file before me on the softer grassy verge.

The November sun had dropped below the hill, the

residual glow tinting the sky and barely moving water, corresponding shades of pink and apple green, the evening scented with dying leaves and the smoke from the peat fire burning on our hearth. It was a townsman's idea of complete country peace.

Aloud and with great feeling I began to recite appropriate lines from Gray's *Elegy*. I had just wound the herd slowly o'er the lea when I stopped and stared, unable to believe my senses. Bluebell, insisting on her right of precedence as usual, had belted the wath gate so hard that the hook which held it open, lifted. Thus unrestrained the iron gate started to swing shut and Cleverclogs, obstinately trying to squeeze around it, was once more performing a spirited *entrechat* before plummeting like a bathysphere to the bottom of the river.

5   Overture to winter

A sound that was becóming increasingly familiar at Westwath was the cacophonous clash of buckets smiting frost-hard ground. It drowned — which to me was of more consequence — the thump of my body doing the same thing. Sometimes the milk-pail would be full and the contents, tipping out, would freeze in a crystalline lake on the flagstones and make them more slippery than ever, then I would skate over it in the dark with feeding buckets strung along my arms like bangles, and fall crashing to the ground again.

Loaded up for the night-time chores with milk-pail, cows' feeding buckets, calves' feeding buckets, hurricane lamp and torch, Gordon said I looked like a walking tagarine shop, and what did I do for an encore? Another pratfall usually.

I always hung the lamp on a big hook screwed into a

smoke-blackened beam in the cowhouse and used the torch to light the way to the hayshed and doghouse where I measured out nuts and barley from lidded bins into the various buckets. One night as I fed the calves in a pen beneath the hayloft the torch beam picked out a small but concentrated spattering of bird-droppings. Above, the hayloft floor was composed of narrow poles packed with crumbling brown bracken, and a tiny, white bottom was all that could be seen of the chaffinch snuggling head first into that warm haven. Very vulnerable it looked too.

We kept coming across these little snuggeries in the most unlikely places. A clay pipe laid as an air vent through the cowhouse wall was the winter home of a sparrow, and the narrow slot above the runner on the henhouse's sliding door was another but, sadly, we did not suspect this until, one night, we slammed the door shut and a sprinkling of feathers attracted the torch light upwards. We were so sickened and upset that none of us would voluntarily shut up the hens for weeks afterwards.

The cows stayed inside all the time now. Ever since the day I drove them into the garage field and went off to the village to buy a roll of wallpaper.

It was drizzling slightly when I set off but before I had gone far it was raining stair-rods which ran straight off my macintosh and into my boots, and created busily flowing streams on the road itself. No friendly vehicle overtook me and as I trudged the three mile return distance the rain gave place to sleet. Long before I was half-way home I was walking on inner-soles of water which bubbled up between my toes with a most extraordinary sensation. Also before I was half-way home I became aware of familiar voices floating up from the valley.

Heavens, the cows! I had forgotten about them. They really ought not to have been out in weather like this. As far as I could see through the curtains of sleet our neighbours' fields on the opposite hillside were empty, their herds snug and dry in the byres. Our herd was up at the top gate shouting for the RSPCA man and inviting the neighbourhood to witness their treatment. The noise increased when, dragging waterlogged feet, I hove into view. Clearly, they were accusing me of turning poor defenceless animals out to freeze while I gadded off enjoying myself.

For all I hadn't met a soul on the road I knew our cows' genius for drawing an audience out of the air and started to worry that someone who didn't know me might come along and believe them, so I hit the nearest bottom with the shopping bag and told the poor waifs to go down to the cowhouse.

They walked half a dozen yards then turned and walked back to the gate again. I clouted another rump with the same result. Bluebell, as usual, was spokesman for them all. They didn't want to go *inside,* she bawled, saliver stretching like elastic from upper to lower jaw. Just across the road to the top field. Where it wasn't raining.

All right, I was wet and hungry too but, unlike them, I intended doing something about it. I went home for a coffee but half an hour later with the sleet as bad as ever and the girls still complaining I put on a dry waterproof and went to bring them in.

The beck had risen higher than I had expected in that short time and was already flowing quickly over the wath. I scooped a few nuts into the cows' buckets and set them in their troughs in the cowhouse. This would induce them to lower their heads which was a help when fastening their chains. Then I waded across the wath and called them in.

They didn't come. They stayed pressed against the top gate as though chained to it. I told Jess to fetch them down. Jess looked at me doubtfully. She wished I'd make up my mind. The last time she had fetched them in early I'd been cross, hadn't I? Well, all right then, but I needn't blame her, that was all.

With the dog behind them the cows trotted briskly down to the beck and stopped dead at the wath. They looked aghast. Surely I didn't expect them to cross *that.* They had done so many times before, I reminded them, and splashed through it again myself, in encouragement. Apparently they thought it was all right for *me* with my boots on, and before Jess could blink they had darted into the field and up to the top gate again.

What had she *told* me, whickered Jess, and bounded after them. I ran to the cowhouse for a bucket of nuts with a notion of enticing them from the near side — cajolery being preferable to violence — and when I returned, there they were jibbing at the water again.

This time I could hardly blame them. The depth and force of the waterfall sweeping over the wath and churning into the beck at the other side was enough to put Stoney Flatt Foss to shame. I knew that if the cows didn't cross that minute they never would. As I was thinking that and rattling my bucket of nuts like a Salvation Army lass with her tambourine they jolly well broke away and headed for that damned top gate again.

It was then that I noticed the Waterboard men. Sheltering in their little caravan, peering out at the rain which was turning their latest excavation into yet another duckpond, their day brightening suddenly as I and my circus troupe went into our routine — the inevitable, enthralled audience conjured up by those pesky cows.

That settled it. I waded determinedly to the other side and as Jess brought the troupe galloping down the track, I blocked off the way into the field, and — the bucket having proved a dead loss as a bribe — I beat it with a stick instead and *scared* them into the water. Then we all waded through it — legs crossing and recrossing like expanding trellis owing to the pull of the current — to the farmyard where, carefully not looking in the direction of the caravan, I sauntered nonchalantly behind the last cow trying to look as if playing 'tig' in a downpour whilst carrying a bucket like a handbag, was a perfectly normal thing to do. Which for me, I suppose, it was.

Since that episode the cows had occupied their respective stalls night and day, wallowing in straw and hay and happy as sandboys — when they thought we weren't looking, but bombarding us with black looks when they knew we were. They twisted around on themselves in the constricted space until they were u-shaped, demanding to be set free in the top field which they still believed to be the Promised Land.

It was worse when we had someone with us because then, as well as keeping on about being shut in, they would, without a qualm of conscience, make out they were half starved as well. Our town friends probably believed that — cows' pelvises being what they are. Will Arrowsmith and the roadmen knew better but I didn't realise this at first. They kept telling me that the cows were 'ower fresh', and interpreting this to mean they were too thin — a belief the cows enthusiastically encouraged — I stoked them up with more hay, nuts and barley until one day Will, with good humoured exasperation said, Good God, what did I feed them on? They were *ower fresh!* And I learned it was local parlance for 'too fat'. I'd been a bit ower savage with the nuts, said Will reprovingly. The cows, of course, didn't agree, but even they had to admit that the u-shaped position was tighter than ever. Served them right if they stayed like it, I told them.

Then it was Christmas Eve and everything in the cowhouse was different. Not in any physical way — I was still reluctant to leave the comfort of a log fire and face the dark, searching cold outside. I still skidded and slid and clashed buckets, and as usual, feared for my ribs as I forced them between the walls and the cows' bellies to dump food under their noses. But something *had* changed. There was a new sense of uplift, a heightened awareness, the knowledge that my surroundings wouldn't be so very different from that stable long ago. There must have been the same animal warmth, the same sweet animal smell, the same sounds of animals breathing, chewing and rustling hay. Even the light would be similar — the soft glow of burning oil. I gave sincere thanks for that moment of sharing.

Crouching on the low three-legged stool next to Bluebell I gave myself up to an orgy of carol singing. By the time I had finished Blue and Rhoda and moved on to Rosie it was to find that she — a notorious one for holding back her milk and thus forcing us to fight for every drop — had been so transported by my singing that she had already let it down and flooded the floor.

Who said that cows are musical?

6 Mush! Mush!

Everything was different on Boxing Day too, because we were snowed up — or at least, were about to be.

We awoke that morning to a furious blizzard which shocked us because Christmas Day, though cold, had been brilliantly sunny and cloudless. After a wonderful dinner which had included vegetables from our garden, Will Arrowsmith's potatoes and Charley Rawdon's goose (we had hens and ducks of our own, but dash it, we couldn't eat our friends), we had walked in the tawny bracken which contrasted so vividly with the gentian blue sky. When we came downstairs on the morning of Boxing Day, criss-crossing snowflakes were hissing against the windowpanes and the ground was already covered to a depth of a couple of inches.

The hens were surprised too, and blamed us for it, but while they had hysterics under the hayloft, the ducks, always glad of an excuse for an expedition, set off to look for the South Pole, their footprints like strings of little kites tailing out behind them. On and off throughout the day, they could be seen in convoy like a fleet of tugboats importantly chugging through the fine dry snow which parted about their breasts like bow-waves. When they weren't trecking through Antarctic's icy wastes, Annabelle, Annabelle, Annabelle, Annabelle and Jemima with their husband, Sir Francis, were crowded on the narrow strip of water remaining to them between the icefloes on the beck, earnestly comparing notes and discussing their next sortie, which they then carried out with great solemnity.

Rupert, Sydney and Uncle Simon, the three stirks who

had been too young to let out into the calf field in autumn and would now have to remain inside until spring, watched the ducks with envy. That white stuff falling like manna from the heavens was obviously eatable — and people out there were actually walking on it. Following the example of Uncle, who in this fashion regularly drank rainwater pouring out of the gutter on the roof in preference to that in his bucket, Rupert and Sydney leaned over the pen half-doors and caught what they could on great, long anteater-like tongues.

That afternoon the Castle Park children joined ours and sledged in the garage field. Pauline reminded me how much I had enjoyed the lorry ride and invited me to share her sledge so it was unfair of her to blame me when she kept falling off the back. It seemed that we dragged the sledges to the top of the field twice as often as we sped down it, shoving off in a flurry of snow, steering with binder-twine lines and a considered touch of an out-flung heel as we judged the exact moment to veer away from the beck, leap over one hummock and decelerate to a gentle halt in another, way down behind the garage. It was years since I had enjoyed myself so much (there were no hills in our home town) and we kept it up until teatime.

Next day the snow was deeper and still falling. Long after his usual time the postman arrived, close on the wheels of the snow plough. He had an unsettled look about him as he warmed his hands around a mug of tea and reported on conditions over the moor.

By Jove, it was rough on top, he said. The snow was drifting in as fast as the plough made a way through it. It was coming down that blinking thick he couldn't see through it. 'I tell you,' he said grimly, 'I came over Bleak Howes by instinct!'

He had no more deliveries that couldn't wait, he said, and was off back to town while he stood a chance.

The butcher's wife telephoned. Mike and Ken, his brother, had set off with the meat but she couldn't say when they would get there. As their journey covered the same route as the postman's I thought it unlikely that they ever would. I didn't say so as she sounded worried enough already. She rang at ever shortening intervals as the day wore on, sounding more and more distracted. I didn't blame her. I was worried enough myself, and hoped that they had turned back.

After each phone call Gordon and I, putting on our Captain Scott hats, would plunge out into the blizzard to see if there was any sign of them. We didn't expect that there would be. We believed it impossible that anyone could drive through that solid white, stinging curtain which concealed everything beyond arm's length. But our butcher did.

At a quarter past eight in the evening we made one last foray up to the road and there, leading to the hut by the top gate, were vestiges of footprints, and inside the hut was our meat. How Ken and Mike did it I'll never know. They were the last to negotiate that road for a week.

That night, as if wind, snow and hailstones the size of mint imperials weren't enough it thundered and lightened as well, and next morning the general level of snow was over the windowledges. We were shocked when we opened the back door and were confronted by a cliff of snow bristling with splintered wood and huge shark fins of jagged glass. The elderly, arthritic porch, unable to support the extra weight, had totally collapsed.

A fine time we had clearing that, after which we had what had become the daily chore of clearing a path to the cowhouse. It was getting to be more like a tunnel than a path — one long main one leading from the back door down the path and *over* the gate, turning sharp left to the cowhouse door, stopping at doghouse, calf pens and all stations in between; and a subsidiary line striking off down the yard to the hens' quarters. We might well have been on rails as it was practically impossible to deviate left or right.

The wind dropped and there was no more snow overnight. We awoke to a cold, calm, utter silence.

It was a novel sensation, this knowledge that we were completely cut off from our neighbours, a tiny island in an unnavigable white sea. Quite exciting, really, until someone laughingly said, we wouldn't have to break a leg, any of us, would we? Whereupon mother got all worried and said, what about if we needed to call the vet? That sobered us a bit because it would be just like our lot to need the vet at a time like that. Optimistic notions about the possibility of the plough getting through now that the blizzard had stopped were stifled at birth when a kind soul, phoning from the village to enquire after our welfare, told us that the plough had cleared a way through the village but had stuck just by the church and couldn't go any further. There was no way out of the village in any direction.

At least, if we couldn't get out of Westwath, now that the snow had stopped falling we could look around and enjoy the beauty and novelty of it all.

The sunken path to the footbridge was another tunnel roofed with hefty snow-depressed boughs of the great yews which overhung it. The surface of the beck was quilted with white cushions, faint veining here and there merely indicating that water still stirred beneath. In the garage field the snow was thigh deep, and I kept overend only by hanging on to Gordon. Where the road was, was anybody's guess because the walls had completely disappeared. Field, walls, road and the top fields on the farther side lay under an unbroken sweep of snow lifting smoothly to the skyline as if they had been engulfed by a tidal wave frozen in action. Soaring breakers arrested in motion like those on a photograph seemed perpetually on the point of toppling, and trees were the foundation of fantasy shapes sculptured apparently out of salt.

With our eyes lifted up to the hills, we failed at first to notice the phenomenon right under our noses — a series of holes connected by slurring grooves meandering uncertainly along the approximate route of the roadway.

'Footsteps!' I yelled, 'Hey, Gordon, footsteps!' Mr Crusoe couldn't have been more surprised.

Gordon circled round them like an Indian Scout, slanting them against the light. He screwed up his eyes and viewed them again from the opposite side. 'This,' he said solemnly, 'is the spoor of two men with sticks.'

I was impressed. 'You are sure they are not woozles?' I said.

Gordon shook his head. 'Two men,' he repeated. 'Walking in the direction of the cattle-grid. They walked *up* the hill then —' he paused impressively — 'they came down again. *Walking in their own footprints!*'

I clapped my hands in admiration and amazement.

'The question *is*,' he went on, 'who were they?'

'It was me Dad and George,' piped up a familiar voice. 'Went up to the pub last night.'

Pauline's colourful appearance was hardly less startling than her announcement. Her legs were encased in green plastic fertiliser bags, criss-crossed Celtic-fashion with binder twine. Over her coat she wore a tabard made from another plastic bag — a yellow one — with holes cut out for head and arms, the tradename emblazoned upside down across her chest in an elegant arc, and on her head was a blue woolly pompom hat pulled well down over ears and eyebrows exposing only an enormous grin.

'Thought I'd come down in me Dad's footprints and see how you're getting on,' she said. 'In't it a job?'

We agreed that it was, just. And how were things at Castle Farm?

'Ooh, well, milk waggon hasn't been for days. Me Dad's fair hopping. We've filled all milk churns, scrubbed out them old water tanks and filled them, me Mam's buckets and washing-up bowls and now we're putting it in t'bath!'

'Heavens. It's to be hoped the waggon gets through soon.'

'Aye', said Pauline seriously and pronounced a phrase that has become a family saying, used over the years whenever a sticky situation crops up. 'Ah dean't knaw what t' mak o'job ah's seer.'

Robert and Antony were bowled over by the magnificence of Pauline's rig-out and had to have outfits like it. We have a rather washed-out photograph of the three wierdly, although admittedly sensibly, dressed children, shuffling up the snow-banked garden path in single file, and strung out in an endless line behind, five ducks, one drake, one cockerel and twelve hens, like the Children of Israel crossing the Dead Sea on their way to better things.

Gordon spent the afternoon making a sledge. A big one

for transporting things. He called it the Flying Bedstead because its chief component was an old-fashioned convertible bed-chair. We used it that evening to lead a few bales of straw from the stack which was gently disintegrating up by the Browns' house. Straw had always been delivered there because of the difficult approach to our inconveniently sited farm and we had been so thoroughly brainwashed by Westwath's former owner that we didn't, for some years, put our minds to arranging anything better.

It was an ethereal moonlit night — all silver, white and grey. From the top of the stack we had a privileged panoramic view of the scene. It was like a Japanese picture on white cartridge paper, the sheep-beeld a mere suggestion sketched in grey, the sparse neighbouring farmsteads exquisitely drawn in Indian ink.

It was mid-morning on New Year's Eve when the brittle silence shattered with the sound of a tractor engine.

'It's me Dad,' shouted Pauline, who, squeezing every last ounce out of her father's footprints, was visiting us again. 'He said he was going to try and get to t'village today. We've nowt else to put milk in.'

We stood outside and listened. Laboriously the tractor struggled up the one-in-four and faded in the distance.

'He's done it,' we all cried excitedly.

Overjoyed, Gordon and I collected Jess and the Flying Bedstead and made a bid for freedom and tinned tomatoes which, because of recent unobtainability, had become obsessionally desirable. We stumbled uphill, Gordon in one of the tractor's deep, sharp-edged tracks, Jess and I in the other. Big as she was, Jess couldn't see over our groove at all. Her horizon was bounded by the back of my boots but she was as pleased as we were to be up and doing something at last.

It wasn't an easy walk. Sometimes we tripped over our own narrowly confined legs and belly-flopped into yielding boot, sleeve and collar-filling coldness. The higher we climbed the deeper it got. Up on the exposed moor where nothing impeded it the wind had run amok, evidence of its passing manifest in an assortment of practical jokes —

natural hollows had been filled in and built up to create rearing eminences, and ridges and outcrops reduced to the status of valleys. The tall signpost that stood at the end of the long, narrow road which leads to the head of the valley was buried to the full height of its stem, its wooden finger resting on the white sheet and pointing the way to nowhere.

On and on over this fantastic landscape wavered the double scar, blurred at intervals by discoloured dollops of compressed snow gathered and dropped during the tractor's progress, and on and on we floundered in it getting hotter and hotter with each step.

I began to imagine that I was a legionnaire struggling across the Sahara with no water and the fort another fifty miles away. My eyes were dazzled. I squeezed them shut for a second to rest them and when I opened them again there was a man on a bike.

'Gordon,' I said, 'there's a man on a bike. I think it's a mirage.'

At that moment either the mirage exploded or the man fell off his bike; there was nothing to see but snow and tractor tracks merging on the horizon.

'Sunk without trace,' said Gordon after an interlude when nothing seemed to happen. But he was wrong. There *was* a man and he was walking now. It was John Metcalf, the caretaker of the Roman road, stumbling along one of the grooves, his balance direly threatened by several indifferently wrapped loaves which he clutched to his bosom.

He couldn't be trying to get to the Roman road, surely? we asked him. We knew that he spent his days weeding, tidying and generally looking after it, sheltering when necessary (and I should think that would be pretty often considering its position right on top of the high moor) in a curious little stone hut. But honestly, wasn't this carrying devotion to duty too far?

He laughed. No, he wasn't going up *there*. Only as far as the Youth Hostel with the bread.

We continued to look incredulous because the Youth Hostel was a mere stone's throw from the Roman road, both of them a good mile along that now totally obliterated road indicated only by that crazily inviting signpost. John thought our amazement was due to the existence of the bread, and proceeded to put us in the picture.

The siege, it seemed, was over, and there was bread in the village at last. It had been brought by a helicopter which had landed first at the shops and then by the church, and was still there with a TV cameraman filming everything. We continued villagewards and found John's cycle close by the church, dumped in an Everest of tumbled snow-boulders. The snowplough's — geographically to juggle a bit — Waterloo.

We climbed over the boulders and there at the other side, sitting by the church as John said, was the helicopter, a big, yellow leggy insect flown in from another planet. By gum I was chuffed.

We left the Flying Bedstead lying trustingly beside it and swaggered vain-gloriously along the village street and into the shop, hoping everyone knew we had been marooned up in them thar hills for a week and were therefore as interesting as the Men who Won the West.

The shop had bread and tinned tomatoes but very little else. Pan scrubs and packets of wild-bird seed well spaced out along the shelves did their best to keep up morale, but it wasn't the same.

It was the hotels, explained the shopkeeper. They were still full of stranded Christmas guests. The poshest one, she confided, had rationed its visitors to one slice of bread per meal and was feeding them exclusively on frozen chicken and fish fingers.

Outside the shop we ran into Will and George and the tractor. The disposal of their milk might have been the reason for the trip but the pub hadn't been forgotten. They had made sure that it was still functioning despite the weather and promised it a return trip that night to welcome the New Year.

They greeted us very cheerfully. 'Hast tha got all tha wants?' cried Will. 'Get in, then. Tha can have a lift back in t' transport-box. Move ower, Shirley, lass!'

We looked doubtfully at the transport box which was

attached to the back of the tractor. It was the shape and size of an orange-crate and contained two large oil drums, half a dozen cartons of provisions, two snow shovels and Shirley Denby who lived at a farm away beyond Will's and had been stuck in the village since Boxing Day.

We re-stacked the boxes, altered the angle of the shovels, pushed Jess off Shirley who was fast subsiding beneath her, wedged her in another corner and insinuated ourselves in the cracks. George sprang up and stood inside the cab by Will's shoulder and with a protesting shudder the tractor started forward.

Our progress would have left Ben Hur cold but it heated us up all right. Especially the bit where we left the apron of common which fronted the shops and took a flying leap over the Pennine Range thrown up by the snowplough.

The helicopter still squatted by the church but now, across the road outside the Waterfall Hotel, TV cameras were busy. They were filming the marooned guests who were bravely being good sports and laughing gaily as they kept their peckers and tankards up.

None of the journey, so far, had approached luxury standards; what with the extraordinary suspension of the transport box which not only jolted up and down but shook from side to side, the cargo occasionally shifting and dominating the passengers, Jess refusing to budge from what she considered the best position for abandoning ship in case of wreck and consequently the rest of us having to mould ourselves around her — we had forgotten about the Himalayan ridge which had daunted the snow plough. So when George called to us to owd on we were coming to the rough bit we were surprised because we thought we had been having it.

Not so. While we clung to each other and more stable bits of tractor the transport box achieved several new positions which surprised even Will. But we made it, and a couple of days later the snow plough did too.

7 A winter's tale

And so the winter ground on and although, as people told us, it was not to be compared with that of '47 when the village was completely cut off for a couple of months and outlying farms even longer, we were not greedy and were prepared to put up with a mere two or three days incarceration every week or so. This usually occurred over a weekend or half-term holiday, a mischance that annoyed the boys for a good fall of snow on weekdays often meant enforced absence from school.

The Young Wives' Children's Christmas Party, cancelled during the Christmas week imprisonment, was held at last in the February half-term holiday. Walking home afterwards against the blizzard was like swimming in a goldfish bowl full of milk in which the smudged outlines of Castle and Ellers farms floated like drowned moths. Dense snow filled in our footsteps as soon as we made them and Robert, Antony and I were the last to walk along the road for three days.

It kept on snowing and we kept on clearing paths down to the previous hardened surface, not realising how much higher than normal this was until very much later when the snow had almost gone and I wanted to peg out a few clothes. The last time I had done that I had left the peg bag hanging on a snag on the cherry tree at waist level. Now, to my surprise I found that the snag was way above my head.

Some days the sun shone and melting snow ebbed slowly away from roof ridges but this only served to lengthen the icicles which fringed everything. There were mornings when they hung from the cowhouse eaves right down to the ground, constructing a formidable portcullis over the door which, according to the cows, was just part of the general plot to keep them in.

But the cowhouse icicles were nothing compared with those in the Scar, the ravine which bounds part of our land. There the sheer rock face was a frozen cascade of them, most having the girth of a cow and many attaining a length in excess of twenty feet. They hung there like sets of organ pipes, an effect heightened when the lung-freezing wind hummed through them.

Beneath that encasing ice were the rock walls which, until a few months before, had been the playground of our flock of Swaledale crossed with Scottish Blackface sheep, and on which Gordon and I had performed spectacular mountaineering feats as we rescued over-ambitious small lambs stuck fast on pencil-slim ledges.

The one winter we had experienced as shepherds had been bad enough, the snowbound moor offering no sustenance to the hungry sheep whose backs seemed permanently encased in a carapace of clinging snow. As I distributed sugarbeet pulp, hay and sheep nuts along the trods I had been almost flayed alive by the cutting wind, perforated by hailstones driving in from Siberia and buried waist deep in unsuspected snowdrifts, so I was more than thankful that we had parted with the flock the following autumn. I was glad to be spared the struggle and heartache of other farmers, many of whose flocks were decimated by the end of winter. One man died while searching for his buried animals. Yet there were remarkable cases where sheep had survived for two or three weeks beneath enormous drifts having eaten the wool off each other's backs. How they escaped suffocation is beyond me.

Sheep, then, were not my problem but I had other things to worry about. Me, for instance. I had carried so many buckets of water at four gallons a time from the tap in the kitchen — which was the nearest unfrozen one — to the trough in the calf field, that my shoulders had dropped to where my elbows used to be and my hands were flapping about my knees. King Kong, had he dropped in (and come to think about it that is about the only misfortune we haven't had to contend with) would have welcomed me as his mother.

The water in the cowhouse still flowed, thank goodness. This was particularly lucky for me because there it was needed for more than just drinking. To pay me out for confining them inside, Rosie, Rhoda and Bluebell kept me continually cleaning up. Over their shoulders they watched me shovel, sweep and swill until the grip was as spotless as a sea-washed shore, then just as I was about to go through the doorway they would squeeze themselves in a supreme effort and deposit a row of splodges like misshapen sand pies.

Whenever possible — that is after a visit by the snow plough — I would call Jess and we would do a Nanook of the North away up the road. This was purely for exercise because even where we could see over the high white cliffs carved out by the plough, our eyes met nothing but more snow which, as scenery, palls after a month or two.

Neither did we ever see anyone to pass the time of the day with until, on our way home one day, we met a mouse. Jess saw it first because I happened to be walking with my eyes closed at the time. When I opened them and looked around for her she was standing interestedly regarding a small black dot. The mouse, I saw when I retraced my steps, was staggering along at the foot of the endless snow cliff with a 'the U.S. mails must go through' expression on its face until, becoming aware of Jess at last, it tried to change course, went vertically up the precipice and fell backwards in a shivering heap an inch from Jess's enquiring, shiny black tipped nose. When I picked it up it sat in my palm with its eyes tight shut and resigned itself to its fate. The Pony Express had, for once, failed to complete a mission. I carried it back to the wall of our top field and poked it in between the stones. There in the dry dark was guaranteed food and a soft bed thanks to the strong winds of last haytime which drove the drying grass against and into the boundary wall. Dessicated grass and hayseeds still lodged in the crevices deep inside. It would have been hard to find more luxurious lodgings, and whatever Binnie Brown says now, I maintain that it was *not* the same mouse that she found nesting among Steven's shirts the following spring.

All winter snow stories abounded; some tragic, many

amusing, but it is the latter we remember.

Our shopkeeper told how he and Dick Harrison had been gritting for a motorist on a steeply climbing road. 'Dick got into the boot of the car to add a bit of weight. Off they went. I stood and watched, expecting feller to stop and let Dick out at top of the hill. But no. On they went right out of sight. In the end I had to drive after them and there was Dick trudging back right up on top moor road. "Let you off in the end, did he?" I said. "Did he Hell," grumbled Dick. "I had to bale out or I'd have finished up in Whitby." '

Gordon had plenty of tales to tell. His 'Gather round while I tell you a snow story' was a nightly, magnetic invitation. He would set off for work in conditions so appalling that I expected never to see him again. Sometimes, of course, he didn't get there. If the roads were impassable he would have to come back, usually complete with car but occasionally not. At these times he would wait until the next day, or whenever the weather allowed, and return on foot to whichever snowdrift was holding up the proceedings. Blocked roads were general and buried vehicles commonplace, though one driver digging out his mini was shattered to find another one buried underneath.

At 9.15 one February night I, with culinary *éclat*, was stirring hot water into Gordon's dinner which was drying up on the Rayburn, when the phone shrilled. The car was stuck fast in the next village, reported Gordon. He was setting off to walk and, by golly, he was hungry. As his position was four miles east of home, three of them across lackadaisically fenced moorland, I judged that there would be time for me to concoct an entirely new meal with all the trimmings before he was ready to sit down to it.

An hour later, booted and duffle-coated, I put Jess to bed in the doghouse, checked the cows' bedding and the stirks' water and fastened everybody up for the night, seeing nothing beyond the heavy hanging drapery of falling snow. My mind's eye saw Gordon stumbling off the unmarked road on to the uncharted moor, falling foul of unseen rocks and pitching into snow-drowned gullies. By the time I had got him in a crevasse with a broken leg, snow settling uncaringly over his unconscious body, I could stand it no longer and set forth to look for him.

Find Gordon! I couldn't even find the road bridge. I had crossed it all right but its chest-high parapets being all one with the level of the road, it had, in effect, vanished. If a bridge in the comparative shelter of a valley could do that what chance had an unprotected traveller in the open wilderness 'on top'?

My imagination was churning away in its usual alarmist manner and it was some time before I realised that the voices that had been impinging for the past few minutes were not the last despairing cries of my husband but the homely tones of Will Arrowsmith and his sister Frances, who, I saw when I rounded the corner, were shouldering the wheels of a small van, slewed at a violent angle across the road. As I drew near Will left the van and climbed up on to his tractor and began what was obviously not his first attempt to drag the van free. Frances went on pushing her wheel and I shoved at the other and inch by slippery inch, we all tacked up the hill.

At the top Will stopped. Frances and I picked ourselves up, shook off the loose snow, draped ourselves over the van and panted.

'Hallo,' said Will, peering through the blizzard and apparently noticing me for the first time, 'what's tha doing oot here, then?'

'Thought you were Gordon,' I gasped.

'Gordon? What's *he* up to? Ain't he home yet?'

I told him the gist of the telephone message. 'And I was just going to look for him when I heard you. It must be more than two hours now, since he rang.'

'He'll be OK. Likely I'll pick him up. I want to see Frances gets home all right.' Frances lived in the next village and if Will's tractor got him as far as that I was pretty sure that Gordon's deliverance was nigh. My faith in Will is unshakable even to this day.

I returned home in a better frame of mind. Westwath lay cocooned and all but inaccessable. Another snow-siege was beginning. At midnight I was stirring hot water into another dehydrated dinner when I was struck rigid by a knock at the door.

I opened it. Smiling ingratiatingly Gordon doffed a snow-caked hat. 'Can ye tell me?' he said in a creditable Scots accent. 'Is this the way to Stoney Flatt Foss?'

8 *Spring's awakening*

It was almost summer when spring shook off the winter blankets. For weeks the postman had trampled a path to our door delivering fistfuls of enquiring letters from would-be tenants of our holiday bungalow, and sitting on the warm drying rail in front of the Rayburn I sifted the oats from the chaff. Usually there is far more chaff than oats and that year was no exception. Highly scented, thick, pink deckled-edged paper asking the *number* of bathrooms in five words to a page; parties of twelve requiring at least four bedrooms; and a plea from a schoolmaster that the television should be a colour one. Hurriedly I put him out of his misery. No TV at all. In fact, no electricity.

I had been amazed to learn during those early days what great store people set by television. On learning that we existed without electricity visitors would look aghast and cry, 'But you'll have no TV.' One bungalow family brought a portable set with them and spent the best part of the week trying to get reception with the aid of wire and car battery, both borrowed from us. 'We like the telly,' explained the head of the family, 'because it learns you fings.'

So, dear Sir, I reply, I am so sorry but I am afraid there is no etc. etc. What I should really like to say is, why do you need it, when you come to a place like this?

Peer out through the west windows of the bungalow and you will see — beyond the knotty fruit trees into whose branches red currant bushes of incalculable years climb to incredible heights and hang festoons of translucent beads (trees whose names alone are worth a few minutes of your time; Queening, Squaring, Royal George, Leathercoat, Bloody Butcher, Flowery Town to mention a few) — cattle quietly grazing.

In the pint-sized fields subtly-hued oaks, such as Constable painted, stand in pairs. Once there were four such partnerships constituting what must have been a noble avenue, but today, only five stalwarts and three stumps, too decayed to be ring-counted, remain. The cows don't care tuppence for Constable but they are grateful for the trees' shade and the abrasive feel of the bark on necks newly released from winter's chains.

Where rushes take over the marshy field margins a whole succession of entertainment takes place. An opening chorus of vivacious marsh-marigolds hundreds strong is followed by a spectacular danced by milkmaids and ragged robin, with complexions ranging from slightly flushed to blushing crimson. The choreography is arranged by the wind and the whole production is powdered and scented by woodruff and meadowsweet. The flying ballet is a long-running attraction with special appearances by the Prima Ballerina, a heron, on gala occasions.

Come outside through the stable-door of the bedroom and smell the hay in the barn. There's another apple tree there, a Keswick. In autumn the fruit hangs low and Bluebell fastidiously selects the best to crunch on her way into the cowhouse. The Keswick is sugar daddy to a wild rambling rose, a beautiful but hard-boiled floozie who has ruthlessly hoisted herself up by the elbows to the topmost branch and flaunts her hips shamelessly.

The most artistically temperamental member of the cast though, is the beck — a river, really. Wider than our main road. In his quieter moods we can do what we like with him — within reason. He'll allow us to wade, swim, paddle canoes. He is an amiable host to innumerable moorhens, wagtails pied and yellow, mallard duck with peacock-blue medal ribbons emblazoned on each wing and, more rarely, dippers. But when he swells angrily and gets too big for his boots ... watch out!

The backdrop to all this has been painted by a Master Craftsman in moorland and forest tones of every shade of pink, brown, green and red.

Uncaring, in February, about its would-be occupants, the bungalow resembled a squat little man unexpectedly petrified during a shampoo and shave, snow lather dripping into his eyes and smothering his chin, too cold and uninviting yet to attract my ministrations.

But however reluctant to commence business spring was, the calendar inexorably marched onwards and suddenly it was Roger's second birthday and the day when Rhoda was due to calve.

This last event was looming on my horizon like a thundercloud at a picnic because if she threw the calf out into the world like she had done last time I didn't give much for its chances. This year the cows were still inside the byre and not in a roomy yielding field where there was space for calves to be tossed about like cricket balls. Because I could just see the new boy breathing his first and last upside down on his head on the concrete, I packed straw over every inch of floorspace and half-way up the walls. With equal thoroughness the cows ate it, thanking Providence for the bounty. I scattered more straw, unconvinced that even if the calf survived his debut he wouldn't come to grief under the careless feet of his relations, and I haunted the cowhouse with a vague, unformed notion of being there to field the calf when lobbed.

Why botherments never come singly, I don't know, but there I was with a houseful of small children happily entertaining themselves, me icing a Humpty-Dumpty face on a birthday cake with a book on calving a cow propped open beside it, eggs for sandwiches boiling in one pan and a pair of scissors boiling in another. The reason for the scissors was obscure but in books and films people always seemed to be boiling them when babies were due and I wanted to be on the safe side. I hadn't much of my mind on the cake because every few minutes either I was running into the living room to dissuade the host from intimidating the guests, or I was plunging out to the snow-girt cowhouse imagining the worst. Always the cows were eating the carpet, with babies the last thing on their minds.

Roger had just blown out the birthday cake candles and I was wiping spray off the children opposite when Gordon came home. Did I know, he said, that Rhoda had a son and was bathing him while he had his tea? Now, there was no need for me to jump about. Everything was fine.

It was too. The beautiful little Angus bull standing unsteadily on splayed legs was nuzzling Rhoda's udder, already instinctively butting it to release the milk while an exploratory grey tongue lapped about the swollent teat. His mother reached backwards as far as her chain would allow, and uttering low cooing grunts, licked with rasping strokes the sticky mucus off the calf's flanks. Sometimes he lost his bearings and staggered a step or two in the wrong direction and Rhoda called encouraging directions to bring him back to her side.

The next dragging step into spring brought us to Mothering Sunday. A pleasant moment in the church service is when the youngest children present their mothers with little spring posies after first taking them up to the altar to be blessed. As usual, we were all dewy-eyed as the little ones thrust the flowers into our expectant hands, even though only an hour or so before those same hands had been frenziedly scratching the snow in likely places in the hope of finding a few inch-high snowdrops or the odd sessile primrose, while tearful offspring hovered critically complaining that those mingy things were *hopeless*.

Shamelessly pampering me, as always, the family presented me with a pair of immaculate dishcloths and two gleaming new mucking-out forks. It just shows how far we had come from Bellfield Avenue when I tell you I was delighted with the forks. The dishcloths I could take or leave alone.

March was drawing to a close but weatherwise nothing had changed. Gordon still buried the car in snowdrifts; we still spent days cut off from our neighbours and the boys still came in soaked to the skin. One day, to add spice to the situation, the hem of Antony's saturated coat was solid with two inches of ice fringed along its length with embryo icicles. It looked like a Red Indian tunic and I had to thaw it in the oven before it could be wrung out.

But, however unseasonable, Easter was approaching and we could no longer put off the annual overhaul and spring clean of the bungalow. I took down the curtains and rolled up the carpets, and Gordon ripped up a section of floorboarding which was suffering from damp. Then, incredibly, with the suddenness of an explosion, the weather changed.

The heavy quilt of cloud was torn aside and the sun beamed through with astonishing strength. Mercury shot up the thermometer tube like lemon squash up a straw, and we flung off layers of clothing with the abandonment of Gypsy Rose Lee.

From every direction issued the sound of running water. From the whispering of melting icecaps dribbling off the tops of gateposts and percolating down the textured stone, to the gurgle of overfilled gutters spilling down thrumming fall pipes. From the chortle of new-born streamlets excitedly exploring new territory, to the full-bodied bellow of the overfed beck sweeping the last of the icefloes down to the sea. Released from their long supported burdens trees tried out their limbs again and on every side branches were springing back to their rightful places pock-marking the surrounding snow with catapulted waterdrops.

As Noah welcomed the sight of the olive leaf plucked off, we welcomed the emergence of the dead brown stalks of taller plants, and a day or so later the gradual appearance of patches of grassland which grew larger every hour. Thus summoned, we temporarily abandoned the bungalow, called out the whole family — except mother, and started muck-spreading.

It was then, when the bungalow was at the nadir of depression with a dank and earthy-smelling hole in one corner of the floor, untidy piles of planks in another, the cooker standing dead centre of the living room with a roll of carpet hanging chevron-like over it, chairs standing on the table cheek by jowl with a gasfire and breadbin, cobwebs understudying curtaining and beds devoid of all but the springs, that a family of prospective tenants chose to come and view it.

Awestruck, the youngest boy gazed about him.

'It's not like home, is it mum?' he said glumly.

'But dear,' said Mum brightly. 'This is *different*. This is how they live, in the country.'

9 Lofty ambitions

Muck-spreading called for so many helpers because we possessed no mechanical spreader and it all had to be done by hand and my Mothers' Day presents. Gordon and I were the loaders. We heaped the heavy manure on to a sledge which Gordon had made from lengths of corrugated iron sheeting. The sledge was then towed behind the tractor into the fields. There, everybody helped to fork it off again, spreading it as evenly as they could. Sometimes we dodged other people's aim and sometimes we didn't. It was a sport guaranteed to keep us on our toes.

The sun went on shining and more and more ground was appearing until on the Tuesday after Easter, which was freakishly hot, I decided to let out the cows for a bit of exercise.

The second I squashed in alongside Bluebell and laid hold of her chain the cows knew what was about to happen. For all that I had been doing the same thing all winter — that is, squeezing between old Fatty and the wall to reach her food trough — this time they knew it was different. I think they knew before I did. Their eyes bulged with anticipation and as the heavy chain clattered from Bluebell's neck and she backed out of her stall like a smokey old tramp steamer leaving her berth, the other two tossed their heads and marched up and down impatiently. By the time Rhoda was released and going astern Rosie was halfway up the wall with excitement and as her chain dropped I had to do a swift backwards hop into the food trough to escape being scuppered.

She charged outside and butted Bluebell's skull with a clonk that resounded down the valley and was the preliminary to some very spirited head wrestling, to which Rhoda — having horns — was not invited. In any case Rhoda was otherwise occupied. Having deliberately overturned a couple of wheelbarrows and accidentally flattened a bucket she was now scattering hens and food troughs like shrapnel on her way to the open gate of the holme field. There she indulged in an orgy of rubbing and head scratching, demolishing in two seconds flat a willow sapling I had been nurturing for the past year. The next day Spring, trying to run before she could walk, found the whole thing too much for her, pulled up the blanket of snow and the cows found themselves back in the byre again.

It was the second week in May before finally they were released, and though the moors were still streaked white where snow packed the deep gullies and were to remain so for a week or two longer, the grass in our fields had grown sufficiently to command the grudging attention of even our coddled herd. Despite the late season the cuckoo had returned on St. George's Day, as usual, closely followed by the swallows who recommenced building in their accustomed place in the cowhouse. This favoured spot was, wouldn't you know, immediately above my head as I sat milking Rhoda, and it got so that I had to rush through this chore with one eye slanting heavenwards as I dodged falling feathers, hay, flaking whitewash and worse. I should be thankful they didn't build with bricks, was Gordon's response to my complaints.

All this frantic housekeeping made me feel guilty about my own which had been in a state of almost complete suspension since I became a farmer. So I went indoors to see what I could do about the attic. The first good view of our attic at Westwath was a bit of a set-back. I hadn't imagined the all over decor of guano and its accompanying smell. One end, to be sure, wasn't too bad. It had fewer missing roof tiles and the floorboards were covered with faded green linoleum. There we temporarily stacked our spare furniture and cartons of books.

It was the two thirds at the other side of the stair opening which made us gulp and turn green. In 1932 the roof had been lined out with a tough, heavyweight cardboard. The date and name of a previous owner was scrawled in thick pencil on the upper side. The upper side was visible to us because it had torn away from the rafters and been dragged into sodden swags by the weight of birds' nests and droppings, some of it sprawling in undulating sheets over hidden objects on the floor. The smell was overpowering. In those early days when we had so many more urgent claims on our time we had had the roof temporarily patched, cleaned up the worst of the mess and closed the attic door firmly up on it.

When next I opened it, the smell was not nearly so bad and instead of nausea, I had an upsurge of anticipation. After all, this was a *real attic* still containing a stack, yet unplumbed, of relics of the Rusts, the former owners. Carefully, I pulled out from the eaves and began tenderly unwrapping what could only be delicate china ... Sèvres, perhaps, or Chelsea. It was neither. It was bedpans. Two of them. And feeding cups. And some assorted round basins with holes in the bottom for waste pipes. Come the day when we turn the place into a Cottage Hospital they will be our front line. In the meantime I pushed them back into the eaves and as they continued to draw my eyes with morbid fascination, covered them with another *objet trouvé*, a Union Jack.

None of these things really held me but when the meagre light from the tiny glassless skylight revealed the promising bulk of two cabin chests I knew I had hit the jackpot at last. In a fever of excitement I tore back the lid of the first. It was the otherwise empty lair of a well-nourished, supersized spider who skipped agilely out of a corner with his fists raised. I beat him by a short whisker and slammed down the lid. The second chest I approached more circumspectly, suddenly mindful of The Mistletoe Bough. It contained two flat irons, a butter pat, a carpet beater, a pair of what I hoped to be goffering irons but turned out to be curling tongs, and a few other objects of unknown purpose and zero value. I was very disappointed. Not even a faded satin slipper or wilting feather boa. I was cheered briefly by the discovery, hanging on one of the numerous jumbo sized, hand made nails which spiked the great purlins, of the remains of an Edwardian parasol. It had been very beautiful in its time — perhaps it was part of a trousseau — with its cream-coloured lace and frills, but birds and years of damp had been too much for its delicate constitution and it was completely beyond redemption. It was years before I could bring myself to throw it away and there it hung, usually shrouded in cobwebs, evoking a picture of Miss Havisham in her filthy wedding finery every time I caught sight of it.

Another flight of fancy doomed to be dashed to the ground, was the hoped for discovery of a forgotten Stubbs or Rembrandt. Pictures there were in plenty ranging from a large heavily framed early advertisement for Robertson Sanderson's Mountain Dew through large heavily framed early sepia prints of the ultimate in depression, culminating in a large heavily framed photograph of — merciful heavens — the face of the clock at Greenwich. None of these inspired even me in my receptive willing-to-be-pleased mood and I had no hope at all of interesting the National Gallery.

Having cleared the attic of other people's rubbish there was room to spread my own. Not that in my mind it *was* rubbish but opinions differ.

A large carton that had once housed a washing machine was bulging with scraps of material for my patchwork which was known and feared throughout the British Isles.

There was another box full of basket bases and a great coil of cane successfully fighting its way out, relics from another craze. My lopsided woven baskets and bowls had been kindly received by our friends, although now I think about it, the best use for those baskets would have been to hide the patchwork in.

There was a plastic bag of coloured wools in many thicknesses awaiting the blankets I was going to knit for the unfortunates of the world though, as Gordon said, it was a moot point whether they would be unfortunate before or after receiving them, as knitting was never one of my strong points.

There were other relics of past industry. The twenty-year-old dress patterns which might easily become fashionable again. Paints ... boxes, jars and tubes of them. Watercolours, oilcolours, china-painting colours; poster paints and pastels; crayons and charcoal; linseed oil and fixatives. There were tins of hardening barbola paste, odd beads and buttons from jewelry-making days; cardboard, scraps of coloured paper and glue. All this I had smuggled into packing cases when we made the big transmigration from town to country.

For the best part of a week I worked jolly hard rolling up and destroying yards of substantial black cobweb which had been there since before the house was built, scraping off the loosest of the flaking grey limewash and scrubbing the floor. When all was clean the green lino end made a summer bedroom for Robert and Antony, which, if you happened to be ten and nine as they were at that time, was a great improvement on the usual kind. A hurricane lamp swung from one of the outsize nails in the rafters which met at the ridge overhead and the atmosphere was more like Mr Peggotty's upturned boat house than anything. The boys were happy up there and their proper bedroom was freed for visiting friends.

Still in my virtuous housewifely mood I switched my energy to another bedroom ceiling. This was clad with narrow strips of pine which I knew would look fabulous when stripped of a hundred years of dun-coloured paint. But, true to the Westwath tradition which decrees that we have only to launch ourselves into one undertaking for another, more urgent, to rear up and demand attention, it was brought to my notice that Rosie was due to calve any day now and there was no pen prepared for the baby.

Mucking out calf pens was even worse than cleaning the

attic. It was not the smell, particularly — pungent though it was — but the saturated, compressed straw that I was attempting to fork out was always interleaved and held down by the bit I was standing on, so that, in effect, I was lifting myself as well. What with all that lifting and heaving and then having to push the stuff down the yard to the midden in barrowloads because I'm too daft to drive a tractor, by the time the boys came quarrelling home from school I had worked myself into a fair lather. Horses sweat, they say, gentlemen perspire but ladies merely glow. You may call *me* Bucephalus.

However, not only had I been using brawn but my brain had been in motion also and while Robert attacked the calf pen walls with a knife and scrubbing brush and Antony sprayed him and the floor with a hosepipe, I went indoors to check the Artificial Insemination Certificate with my diary and found, as I had begun to suspect, that the A.I. man had mistakenly entered the wrong date and Rosie wouldn't calve for at least another week.

If you are thinking that left me free to return to the bedroom ceiling, I am afraid that you have not been paying proper attention to what I have been telling you all this time. Because now the cowhouse was due for its annual clean and by the time I had swept down, scrubbed and whitewashed that, it was Whitsuntide and our usual Whitsun visitors, the Evanses and Cawkwells arrived for their holiday in the bungalow.

We welcomed them at the gate, exchanged news and laughed heartily about last year when the waterpipe bringing the supply from our spring silted up and for a fortnight, until Gordon and I got it cleared, we — ha! ha! — had to flush the toilets with buckets of beckwater and carry drinking water from the Browns' house. Then our visitors carried their cases into the bungalow and we went indoors for tea.

Still reminiscing about what good sports the folks had been during that water crisis I started slicing bread, and Gordon, trying to fill the kettle from the kitchen tap, said he only hoped their sense of humour was still functioning because, Lord help us, we had got another.

10   It keeps us off the streets

Incredible as it may seem to an outsider (though not, of course, to us who had learned the hard way that complacency was unknown at Westwath and catastrophe commonplace), it was a year to the day since that self-same emergency arose. Suspecting this to be an extreme case of déjà vu we collected together the tank cleaning tools of crowbar, short ladder, buckets and scrubbing brushes and tore a way through the forest undergrowth and up to our neighbour's field above, where our water storage tank was sunk. Our heads full of gloom and fatalistic thoughts we baled out and scrubbed, disconnected the first length of pipe and cleaned it out. But here the story took an unexpected twist because Fate, the old softy, suddenly relented and when Gordon reconnected the pipe and pessimistically flushed it, the water flowed unimpeded, and far down below at Westwath, mother tentatively turning on the kitchen tap fielded a ricocheted jet in the eye. And with that crisis over we had a full day of freedom before the next.

We spent it playing with our new toys. Mine was a four-gallon knapsack weedkiller sprayer and Gordon's a heavyweight chainsaw. These constituted the first brand new equipment we had purchased since coming to Westwath and we were tickled pink with them.

The chainsaw had come on to the strength in the first place to deal with the big elm tree that the flood had washed out of the ground and thrown athwart the beck. The saw, operated with deceptive ease, had ripped the great bole into sections which were heaved out of the water on to the wath and then hauled up and stacked on the bank to dry by guess who? Since then Gordon had spent many a happy hour slicing fallen trunks like swiss rolls, leaving the results where they fell for the help to pick up. On Whit Sunday afternoon he had another orgy, widening his field of activity to include fields, yard and garden: trees, branches and old rotten fencing littered the place like dislocated vertebrae.

It was one of the bits of old fenceposts that sparked off the next crisis.

The usual working partnership of Roger and myself accoutred with sacks and our respective wheelbarrows was following the saw's spoor and working, as Roger said happily, like a snowdrop — Roger at two had a fund of interesting similes; reading like a chimney, and clean as an elephant's door, are another two I recall — when he tripped, put out a hand to save himself and impaled it good and proper on a rusty nail. Gordon prized it off while I fought an attack of the vapours, carried Roger indoors, washed with antiseptic and sticking-plastered the little palm. I quivered with thoughts of tetanus and tried to phone the doctor.

It was our doctor's weekend off. I didn't begrudge him the break. Our family alone must have doubled his work but the delay did heighten the tension.

Apart from calmly reporting that it hurt like a tea-party, Roger took no more interest in the matter but mother, Gordon and I were on tenterhooks until the relief doctor from a neighbouring village rang and called us in to his surgery. Thankfully we hurried down the yard, glanced in passing at the cows who were grazing in the holme field, and nearly had a fit. Rosie, in a corner by herself, a look of extreme concentration on her face, was clearly about to produce a calf.

Reflecting once more on the incidence of multiple tribulations, and wondering why the dickens Rosie couldn't have calved yesterday when all would have been over now (in this, as you will see, I was wrong. Again.) we rushed off to the car. Antony, who was seeing us off, hand't noticed Rosie's attitude. We didn't mention it knowing that he would certainly pass on the news to mother who would have the horrors on the spot.

Mother doesn't like cows. They *look* at her, she says. If it is utterly, inescapably unavoidable that she should pass through a field of them she stares right away in the opposite direction under the ostrich assumption that if she can't see them, then they can't see her.

We didn't know where Dr Robinson's house was, lost precious time looking for it and returned home to find that Antony *had* noticed Rosie's condition and mother was distractedly wringing her hands by the garden gate. We handed Roger into her charge, and happy to be doing something useful, she shepherded him indoors to share a chocolate bar.

Antony was in the field watching Rosie with complete absorption. He was not alone. Binnie and Steven, drawn by the dramatic atmosphere and mother's tremulous phone call, were there too. Steven patently wished he wasn't. He nodded in Antony's direction and threw us a look which conveyed the message that although midwifery was second nature to him, he would do his bit by removing so young a child from the harrowing scene. His face alight with relief he towed the reluctant lad into the wood to look, he said, for wild flowers. Gordon too had vanished and his chainsaw could be heard a very long way off.

Fascinated by the ever wondrous miracle of birth Binnie and I stayed in the background and watched Rosie. A pair of little black hooves first appeared then retracted. They appeared again followed by a sleek wet head. A moment of concentration on Rosie's part, apprehension on ours, and the whole body emerged and hung suspended by the back legs. A short rest while Rosie gathered herself for the final effort, then with a vigorous swing of her hindquarters and a thunk which I could almost feel, she flung the calf to the ground like a sack of coal. And that, as far as Rosie was concerned, was that.

Bluebell and Rhoda galloped up and hovered over the pair like a couple of Mrs Gamps, greeting the newcomer with the full strength of their lungs. He still lay where he had landed in a surprised heap, dazedly suffering the pop-eyed excitement of his elders. Rosie contributed a few yells just for the look of the thing and said Rhoda could have him if she wanted. Not for Rosie the chore of child care. Though the sun was only fitful and a cold wind blowing she made no attempt to dry the calf which was valiantly though unsuccessfully trying to get to its feet.

The effect of the cows' bellows was like that of the 'All Clear' signal and the men emerged from their holes. Steven's wild flower collection was nothing to write home about but we were relieved to see the sack-lined wheelbarrow that Gordon was propelling. In this, the calf was transported to the straw-lined pen where, with sacks warm from the kitchen stove, we scrubbed him dry. Then, with the non-cooperation of Rosie, we fed him with her milk drawn off into a bucket. We bedded Rosie in the cowhouse for the night.

Next morning I found her there, flat out in a coma.

For Bluebell to have milk fever we were well prepared. Bottles of calcium borogluconate and a brand new flutter valve through which to inject it awaited in a drawer of the medicine chest because Bluebell went down with milk fever after calving as regularly as Monday follows Sunday. It was her thing. Her former owner had warned us about it and last year, when we had experienced it for the first time, Will Arrowsmith and George had come to the rescue. But, as far as we knew, this was the first time it had happened to Rosie and it came as a very nasty shock.

Gordon was about to set off for work when I burst into the kitchen. He dropped his lunch bag and ran out to the cowhouse while with trembling hands I gathered together the items for the transfusion.

Gordon attached the bottle of calcium to one end of the rubber tube, upended it and passed it to me. He inserted the needle and the tide of calcium slowly descended in the bottle which I held at shoulder height. After a while I propped up my elbow with the other hand. When the bottle was empty I replaced it with another. I watched Gordon with admiration as he kneaded the liquid into Rosie's flesh. He had learned a good many new skills during the last couple of years.

Shortly after absorbing the contents of the second bottle Rosie struggled shakily to her feet but looked far from well and soon collapsed again. That settled it. I called the vet.

Mr Burn nodded approvingly as Gordon reported what had already been done, produced a flutter valve and more calcium and followed it with a chaser of magnesium sulphate. We watched anxiously, expecting to see the poor animal swell up like a bladder as a result of all that liquid.

All this time she was lying solidly across the cowhouse doorway; Rhoda couldn't get in and was complaining that it was long past milking time. I milked her at last, about eleven o'clock, in the cowhouse annexe next door, tightly slotted in between bales of hay, and about this time Rosie got to her feet again. About an hour later she began pulling at her hay and was soon chewing contentedly in a normal fashion.

And now, said Gordon picking up his lunch bag, he'd get off to work and salvage what was left of the day. Rosie would be OK now and I'd be able to cope all right, wouldn't I? He sounded confident. As he walked down the yard he turned and waved cheerily. Uncheered I drooped indoors and lighted the gas under the potatoes for the midday meal. Intent on holding a blazing bandage under the water tap I was startled by his voice from the doorway.

'Oops, I thought you'd gone. What did you say?'

'I only asked when Bluebell was due to calve?' he said mildly.

I stared. Fancy him coming back again just to ask that! 'In two weeks from now. I *told* you that this morning!'

'You should have told Bluebell.' He gave me a long deadpan look. 'She's just gone and done it.'

One should never give way to hysteria — it's not British or something — so I didn't. I hadn't the strength. Meekly I followed Gordon down the garden path and stared dumbly across the back field. Bluebell, with more than a touch of sauce in her level gaze, stared defiantly back. That, of course, was Bluebell to a T. To take a sticky situation and gum it up properly was her idea of complete fulfilment. She raised her chin, made a mouth like a brontosaurus and bellowed belligerently.

That calf was the smallest I had ever seen. He had not expected to be born for another fortnight or would have made a better job of it. Not that he lacked in anything but size. He was a perfect Aberdeen Angus in miniature and an object of sentimental admiration to everyone except his mother. Knock-kneed and quivering he stood quietly peeping up from under long thick lashes as if unsure of his welcome.

There was no call for the wheelbarrow. Gordon carried the little creature to the pen already occupied by his nephew, and while Gordon cleaned off the mucus and polished up his coat until it shone like black silk, I herded in the excited cow whose disinclination to be tethered at that time of day was overcome by the scent of warm bran mash.

If only she would have allowed her calf to suckle she would have saved me a lot of trouble but that wasn't her way. Bluebell's notion of baby dandling was seeing how far he could bounce. Her udder was enormous. Each teat was swollen to teacup size and shape, and angled like the cardinal points of the compass. Bluebell was getting on a bit and at the best of times her udder was pendulous. Now it barely cleared the floor. To sit on the stool and reach the farthest teat I should have to be equipped with arms four feet long so I dispensed with the stool and milked while kneeling, unconventionally, on the concrete.

I took just sufficient for the calf's meal. A cow's first milk is not like milk at all. It is rich with colostrum: pinkish thick and sticky. Bluebell's milk — because anything Bluebell did was larger than life — was orange-coloured, viscous and gummy as glue. My fingers stuck to the teats, to the short hair of the udder and to each other. When I pushed my own hair back from my forehead it stuck to my hands and tore out in clumps. Cowhair matted my hands so thickly they looked as if they were cut out of felt.

On my way to the house to wash them I was brought to a surprised halt. A regiment of hikers was tramping across the garden with the unswerving purpose of a line of ants. I mustered a pleasant expression and said brightly, 'I'm very sorry but I'm afraid there is no footpath through the garden.' I beamed around to show no hard feelings. After all, I had been lost myself, on occasions.

No one smiled or even spoke. They merely looked through me as if I wasn't there. The only indication that they had noticed me at all was a sort of implied drawing aside of skirts and haughty turning away of heads as they continued up the path, bearing left by the rhododendron. This upset me and I was further annoyed when more and more studded boots clumped down the steps into the garden from the hayfield. I was cooler with this lot. 'There is *no* footpath through here,' I said, dropping icicles with audible chinks. I thought that they were going to ignore me too but a plump individual well kitted out in thick khaki jersey, rolled up shorts, rolled down socks and boots like brass-bound treasure chests, threw me a perfunctory glance, snorted and said, 'Yes there is.'

Following his example his companions — all thirty-nine of them — marched on, eyes to the fore.

I was flabbergasted and hopping mad.

'Now look here, you can't traipse through private property just like that,' I shouted, the strain of the last couple of days getting the upper hand. 'Who,' I said, playing my masterstroke, 'do you think you are?'

Khaki jersey flared his nostrils and tossed his head. 'There is a footpath,' he said deliberately, 'marked on the map.'

'Not through here, there isn't.'

'Yes, there is.'

'Oh no, there isn't.'

'Yes there is.'

'No there isn't. I *live* here so I should know.' Just in time I restrained myself from adding, 'I'll tell my dad. He's a policeman.'

'It's on the map,' reiterated khaki jersey, single-track minded in more than one sense. 'I'll report you to the Ramblers' Association!'

For a while I was too exasperated for words. 'Look,' I said at last, 'just show me your map and I'll tell you where the path really goes.'

'I can't,' he said. 'I haven't got it with me.'

At least he had stopped and was looking at me. He had to. I was jumping up and down in front of him. The lofty stares of some of the others were turning to apprehension as they focused on me properly for the first time and saw me waving *furry hands.*

They went off pretty quickly after that. Khaki jersey brought up the rear following his public footpath through our rock garden. They stumbled hurriedly on each other's heels up the cart track. That's when I counted them.

We let the three cows out to graze for the afternoon. An afternoon marked indelibly by the young son of the new bungalow people. The Cawkwells and Evanses had stayed only for the long Whitsun weekend. The Forests had arrived soon after Tot (as we named Bluebell's son) was installed in his pen. I introduced him to Barry Forest who was not impressed. At his age, an encounter with a baby calf not an hour old, would have set *me* up for a week.

Not that I was really surprised because almost the first words his mother had uttered when I greeted them at the gate was, 'I think a farm holiday is so good for children, don't you? Especially boys.' This last was accompanied by a haunted expression.

This was an opening we had met with before. It was usually — and this time was no exception — followed up by the comment, 'It's so good for them to *run wild.*' (My italics) 'Now just tell me where you don't want him to go.'

At this point my heart touches rock bottom because I know then that anything I omit to specify will be considered fair game, and lacking ESP, I shall be unprepared for the havoc they will wreak in unexpected places.

My eyes drop from mum's eager face to lock with the eyes of her young. We metaphorically touch gloves, spar silently for a moment then retire to our respective corners, the challenger into the bungalow to prepare his attack, myself to the house to consider strengthening our defences.

To be sure, Barry Forest looked harmless enough. He was an attractive child with blond curls and dimples — the lot. Twenty minutes after his arrival he was pelting stones at the ducks — and he was no mean shot. Flowerbeds meant nothing to him. He would as lief kick his football there as anywhere. Dissuaded from that and presented with a choice of fields he chose one not offered, the one where the cows, still in rather a nervous state, were recovering from their confinements. We removed him from there while Rosie, tossing her head menacingly, glared at him the way mother always imagined cows looked at *her*. His balancing feat along the top of a drystone wall brought down the best part of the top course, and he rounded off the afternoon by tramping paths through the long grass in the almost ready for cutting hayfield — already bisected by the road blazed by Khaki Jersey and Co. Admittedly it was a tempting thing to do, a delight only equalled by defiling a sweep of virgin snow. But the hayfield had been a forbidden area determined at the outset.

Rosie's calf, Bruno, was fine and bouncy but Tot, we had discovered, was standing on his ankles with his front hooves turned in. Gordon was massaging the ankles and gently stretching the feet when later that evening Will and George came down to see all our patients. Will was 'fair capped' with Tot. *He* had never seen a smaller one, either. 'He's a bonny lad,' he said. 'You know, an Angus takes some beating for looks.' He thumped Tot's bony skull. 'Aye, he's a grand little 'un. We'll make bee-ast oot av 'im yet.'

'Bluebell hasn't gone down yet,' I said morosely. 'I bet she'll do it about two in the morning.'

Will frowned thoughtfully. 'Aye, she's a bad 'un for that, ain't she. She mun be getting on a bit, though.' He stooped and poked Bluebell familiarly in the udder. 'Got a right bag on her. You could give her a bottle of calcium tonight. It might stop her going down. They say it doesn't, like, but it's wo'th a try.'

We thought so too. After a day like that one, anything that might end it peacefully was worth trying.

11 Emergency ward

Bluebell stood with bulging eyes and smirked as we set up the drip again. Afterwards we left her untied and knee-deep in straw in the cowhouse annexe. If appearances were anything to go by she was much less likely to collapse than we were, so at midnight we went to bed. I awoke in a panic in the early hours, dragged on trousers and jersey over my nightie, sprinted down to the cowhouse and peeped fearfully within. Everything was as normal as could be. I returned to the house, could sleep no more and so started the day like a limp rag. This was hard luck because the day was destined to be a distorted reflection of the last.

Gordon departed for work at the proper time after inspecting all personnel and finding — with one exception — everyone putting on a good face and keeping a stiff upper lip. The exception sat down and gingerly milked the two new mothers, uncertainly estimating the optimum amount that would relieve congestion and discourage mastitis without creating a situation where cows fell down like ninepins with calcium deficiency. My judgement must have been faulty because no sooner had I finished than Rosie became very agitated and unsteady on her feet. Her hooves scrabbled on the floor as if she was skating on marbles and her legs seemed unable to support her. With a hollow groan she sank down and put her head on the ground.

I felt her nose. If she had been lying on her back, feet pointing to the sky and locked in rigor mortis I should still have felt her nose. Ever since that morning last summer when Rhoda, waiting to suckle her calves, had suddenly started blowing like a grampus, her sides heaving in and out until I thought she would burst. When her legs began quivering madly I decided I needed advice. My own legs felt pretty shaky as I set out with the intention of seeking Will at Castle Farm, but was deflected by the sound of voices carrying down wind from the cattle grid. The roadmen, my old allies, I thought hopefully. They might help and were nearer than Will's farm. When I laboured up the one-in-four I found, not Derek and Arnold, but Mr Anderson, a farmer whose stray adjoined ours, calling instructions to his dog which was working amongst the sheep.

He listened carefully while I detailed Rhoda's symptoms, his dog motionless, its eyes a mesmeric influence over the ewes.

'Is her nose wet?' he asked after some thought.

Blankly, I said I didn't know.

'Reckon she'll be all right if her nose is wet,' he said. 'But I can hear Matt yonder. See what he thinks.'

On my way to find Matt, I spotted the roadmen digging out a silted culvert on the road that leads to the head of the valley.

They leaned on their shovels and listened. 'Is her nose wet?' they asked as one man.

I confessed I hadn't thought to look.

'You can usually tell wi' their noses. If noses are wet I reckon there's nowt much wrang wi' 'em,' said Arnold.

'Just seen Matt going down your way,' said Derek. 'Gone to look at his beasts, likely. You'll catch him if you hurry. Perhaps he'll have a look at cow, like.'

I galumphed down the hillside swishing through the scratchy heather, following a narrow sheep track which meandered in the general direction of Mr Stewart's fields. Sure enough, down by the beck, Matt was striding easily across the rough hummocky grazing land accompanied by a number of dogs and half a dozen stirks. I caught up with him close by our joint boundary. I was out of breath myself by this time so reproduced Rhoda's symptoms most realistically.

'Is her -?' he began just as I was coming in hurriedly with 'I'm afraid I didn't notice if her nose was wet.'

'Well,' he said thoughtfully in his slow voice, 'I'll just come and have a look at her and we'll see what's up.'

He followed me over the footbridge and into the cowhouse where I expected to see Rhoda giving her last gasp. Actually she was standing there breathing in the most normal way possible. She was eating hay in a dedicated fashion and at Matt's touch she turned enquiringly and presented a nose that was as beaded with moisture as a newly sprayed leaf. I never did find out what had ailed her.

Rosie's nose was cold and dry. I called the vet.

While I waited for him I went to feed the calves and found them cross-suckling each other, which, as they were both boys, was pointless and bad for them, to boot. So when they had fed I separated the pair of them by partitioning the pen with a short length of fencing. As soon as my back was turned Tot cancelled that out by squeezing through between the bars. He did it, apparently, with no effort at all, but could I push him back again? Could I — as Pauline would have said — heck as. In the end I picked him up and heaved him over the top, which probably did me no good, for although he was small he wasn't as tiny as all that. I narrowed the spaces between the bars with a couple of lengths of wood and one of my awful hammer and nail jobs. Binder twine, in this case, was out because calves like nothing better than to eat it, get it twisted round their insides and expire with the greatest of discomfort.

Mr Burn examined Rosie and diagnosed grass staggers which made a change from milk fever although the treatment didn't appear to be any different. I was becoming quite accustomed to standing like the Statue of Liberty holding aloft 400 cc. bottles.

Bluebell's cleansing retention problem was the next subject for discussion. Really, considering its size and the number of stock at Westwath, our ailment average was pretty good. From a vet's viewpoint, that is.

If Bluebell hadn't cleansed within the week I was to ring him, said Mr Burn, gathering up his paraphernalia and saluting me politely as he left to attend his next case.

As I glanced after his retreating figure the gorge rose in me. There, over the major part of our small garage field a picnic party was in progress. Not just mum, dad and junior, either, but a good dozen people. Those that weren't sitting in camp chairs or brewing up on little gas stoves were disporting themselves, bikini-clad in the beck. It reminded me — except for the bikinis — of the illustration for La Plage in my old French reader. They were not one whit taken aback when I appeared suddenly among them.

Hadn't they seen the notice? I asked, pointing to the square of white lettered blackboard fixed to the iron gate.

'No,' said one man. 'We came over the wall.' Now that I looked at it, it was obvious that somebody had.

'We did see it,' said another man, 'but we can picnic here if we like. It's got nothing to do with you.'

'I beg your pardon,' I gasped. 'That notice says "Private. Road to farm only." '

'Oh, we saw *that*' said the man. 'But we didn't think much of it as a front entrance.'

'Besides,' said the other. 'You don't own it. It's in the National Park.'

For a moment I was speechless. 'Now look here,' I said. 'As a front entrance it's all we've got. There are a hundred square miles of common and moorland up there where you may picnic, and streams you can bathe in. And that belongs to someone too. The Duchy of Lancaster.'

It wasn't a very good exit line but it was the best I could think of, and anyway, it seemed to have some effect. As they started to gather up the cutlery I stalked from the scene.

As I rather shakily returned through the yard I paused to lean on the fence and scrutinise Bluebell. I had been watching her so conscientiously all morning that I was familiar with every saliva trail crossing her back. These were mapped out when she swiped at flies with her long wet tongue. She stared enigmatically back at me, defiantly alert and still firmly planted on all four feet. It was now well over twenty-four hours since she had calved but I ought to have known better than to feel so cheered and optimistic. For, of course, Bluebell was only biding her time. If that brazen Rosie thought that she had stolen her, Bluebell's, thunder this year she had another think coming.

That evening just as we, drooping with exhaustion, were about to take ourselves off to bed Binnie, who had been away for a couple of days, called to ask after the new baby.

'Babies,' we corrected her, bringing her up to date with events, and Gordon, who can't leave well alone, went to take one last look at Bluebell and found her even more cross-legged than we were. At his call, Binnie and I raced to the cowhouse where Bluebell, with immaculate sense of timing, was just crashing dramatically to the ground.

12 Enter Charlotte

Having got even with Rosie you would have thought that Bluebell would have called it quits. But no. She had to go one better. A week passed and still she had not expelled the placenta. I reported to Mr Burn.

'Right,' he said when he arrived shortly afterwards. 'If you would hold her tail ....'

I squeezed in between the wall and Blue, and leaned my back against her, turning my toes safely out of the way, and tussled for possession of the tail. Bluebell stood there smugly, enjoying all the attention.

Mr Burn talked cheerfully as he worked away behind the protection of his waterproof overall. Then suddenly there was a horrid squelching sound and the afterbirth splothered to the ground.

'That's it,' said the vet. 'Its all come away nicely so she'll be all right now.'

When he had gone I eyed the mess apprehensively, wondering what on earth I was supposed to do with it. Immediately my computer brain produced the answer. Nothing.

I sent Bluebell out to graze with the others. Then I scrubbed the feed buckets, setting them on their sides in the sun to dry, and swilled the yard and cowhouse, carefully ignoring the pink, red and purple heap that lay behind Blue's standing. I went indoors, mixed a cake and put it into the oven. I made the beds, washed out a few pairs of socks and pegged them out to dry. The hens were squashed up against the garden gate with their heads thrusting through the slats, a ruff of feathers standing out around each neck. A second layer of hens pressed from behind, and when I opened the gate they all remained for a moment moulded in position like chicken in aspic, until the front ones gave way under the pressure. I scattered some corn and filled their water troughs and turned back to the garden gate.

It was no good. My conscience would not be placated. Fighting every inch of the way, I was drawn back to the cowhouse.

Damn it, I was going to *have* to do something. Gordon wouldn't be home for hours, and flies were already sniffing excitedly in the doorway. Jess, too, was asking earnestly if there was anything she could do to help?

I fetched our largest bucket, set my jaw and tried to pick up the cleansing with a fork. The fork slightly raised one edge of membrane. I stepped over and tried from the other side. The heap lifted, shuddered, gathered to one side and slid off like a jelly. That was that. I could not pick it up with a fork. The alternative appalled me.

For a full two minutes my conscience and I fought a bitter battle as I circled about the suffused mass which clung unhelpfully to the concrete. Then, gritting my teeth and thinking this was a far, far better thing than I had ever done, I gathered the thing hand over hand into my arms and heaved it — and it was surprisingly heavy — into the bucket. The curtain came down on this gory drama when I dug a deep hole — a very deep hole ... Jess was still solicitously glued to my side — at the back of the vegetable garden and tipped the contents of the bucket into it. Since that day I have carried out a number of those interments to the great benefit of the couch grass.

But Bluebell hadn't done yet. No sooner had I rinsed out the bucket in the beck than she started a monotonous mooing which she kept up for the rest of the day, desisting only each time I walked up to her. Then she would stare loftily at me until, making nothing of her, I went away. She started up again in the middle of the night and when I tell you that instead of sending me, Gordon got up and went out to her, you'll know how bad it was. By lunchtime next day I was so fed up with her standing on the holme field hillock imitating a foghorn that I rang the vet again. I had stopped worrying how we were going to pay his bill and started wondering who was going to settle the telephone one.

I poured out my troubles to a fortissimo accompaniment

from outside which, when I held the receiver to the open door, carried clearly over the line. 'She has a sort of pink discharge but I don't think she's in pain. And,' I added brightly just to show how on the ball I was, 'her nose is wet. It's just that she won't SHUT UP! Sorry.'

The discharge was normal, said Mr Burn. He was quiet for a moment then went on to say in rather a helpless tone that he could only think the trouble was psychological. For a second or two I wondered if he was talking about Bluebell or me, but he assured me he meant the cow.

I marched down the field, slapped old moaning Minnie across the rump and screamed, 'If you think I'm going to call in a psychiatrist for you now, you old besom, you've got another think coming. Now BE QUIET!' And believe it or not, she was.

After that — apart from an abortive attempt at retaliation by Rosie who appeared one morning with a swelling like a football on her side, which she said was a growth (Nothing to worry about, said Mr Burn. Only a build up where the calcium was injected which would disappear of its own accord) — we had no more cow trouble until August.

I found time to make curtains and loose covers for the living room and Gordon concreted the floors of some calf pens, both of us working like fury to be done before the next crisis hit us. Haytime came early and hot with the thermometer touching 90°F and despite drawback one, when we all took it in turns to have gastric trouble, drawback two, the fact that it was term time and child labour only available in the mosquito-ridden evenings, and three, a furnace-hot gale blowing up which hurled the haycocks over the top field wall and sent them spinning like tumbleweed along the moor, we did reap a very good crop.

It was during haytime, on Robert's birthday, July first, that he brought home the kitten he had found 'on the front off side suspension' and as it was also the day of Prince Charles's inauguration as Prince of Wales we named it Charles Philip Arthur George. Later we retracted and modified the name to Charlotte Philippa Arthur Georgina.

If there is a feminine of Arthur I do not know it.

I must say it was nice to have a cat — albeit one barely four inches high — about the place again. We had brought three beloved cats with us when we moved to Westwath from Hull, but they were town cats, unused to country dangers, and were with us only briefly before disappearing one by one. Indeed Edward stayed only one night.

We had brought them, sedated, in baskets and they had slept right through until the following day. Then, as Gordon carried in a new Calor gas cylinder, Edward awoke, found himself in strange surroundings and sped past Gordon and up the garden path. Immediately we went in pursuit but he had been absorbed by the unfamiliar territory and we never saw him again.

Small was eight years old, black, white and undersized with a tail like an inverted V — the result of a fracture sustained during a night out with the boys. The evening before we moved he went out to tell them goodbye and returned minus an eye. Small loved the new life and became like a kitten again. The long grass in the hayfield was a happy hunting ground, and a kinked black tail at the head of a wavering line of trembling seedheads was the most we saw of him for days. When I worked in the vegetable garden he sat importantly on an upturned bucket in the gateway and explained to Jess that he was now in charge and dogs weren't allowed. Jess never challenged him but surreptitiously edged her way along the fence until she found a raised corner of the netting under which she could crawl. We never knew the end of Small but he had had seven months of heaven before he vanished. Six months later Treacle-Mustard vanished in the same manner. He was last seen lying full length in his favourite spot on the sunny orchard wall. I combed the countryside around, paying particular attention to the roadside gutters in case he had been run over and dumped, but I never found him.

We had become accustomed to being a three cat household and their departure left a vacuum, therefore — though without admitting it to Robert whom we blame whenever Charlotte's many progeny involve us in some imbroglio or other — we were delighted to have a cat on the strength again. As if we hadn't enough problems.

13   Friends in need

In August our friends, the Wards, came for a fortnight's holiday. Why they keep coming I don't know because we embroil them in something every time.

The range of our emergencies is diverse and infinite. We are seldom without one on hand, the urgency of the current one diminishing solely because of the onset of the next. Mother, indeed, had come to believe that life held nothing else. This, coupled with a slight deafness and immutable propensity for getting hold of the wrong end of the stick, kept her in permanent state of alarm. For example, when Robert, who for months had been publicising his vital need of a model steam engine, lowered his sights somewhat and loped into the kitchen to tell us urgently that he had seen one for twelve shillings and we could buy him that if we liked, mother suspended the washing up, raised her head like a wild animal scenting danger and demanded apprehensively, '*What's* leaking?' Granted Robert was not speaking distinctly, but the point I am trying to make is that she might so easily have been right.

And into this atmosphere of permanently impending doom the Wards — Kath, Denis, Janet and David — descend for what I suppose they must imagine to be holidays. Once I asked Denis why they continued to come. After considering the question a bit Denis said that they had been mixed up in our unlikely affairs so often he guessed they had become as touched as we were.

True, all it needed was for the Wards to arrive and begin innocently unpacking their suitcases and trouble would erupt somewhere on the place. They didn't even have to be here that long. One year they were just coming in at the back door happily calling greetings and saying, goodness, it was good to be back, when the door in the opposite wall, of its own volition, came off its hinges and crashed to the ground under their noses. A typical Westwath greeting that was.

Usually some part of their first day was occupied with accompanying us to the vet's with some canine or feline patient — that is if Mr Burn or his assistant was not already on the farm attending to some animal less portable. Inevitably, Janet and David have grown up believing that this is a standard condition of anybody's holiday.

That year's holiday began with a minor deviation from the norm when Antony, delivering a non-scoring punch with his head to Robert's head, destined Robert to an X-ray on the eye. So that year we began with a trip to the Cottage Hospital instead. Robert cheered up a few days later when his three entries in our local flower and handicraft show all won second prizes. Janet's painting in the class for visitors' children gained a second too. The flowers were beautiful, the childrens' fancy dress parade delightful and we thoroughly enjoyed the day, feeling relaxed and civilised for once.

The next day we were back to normal.

It began when I went out to fetch in the cows and found all three of them in season. And what a performance *that* was. One at a time was always bad enough, but three! And Rhoda, the old faggot, shouldn't have been in that condition at all. She had been served by artificial insemination ages ago. Without Jess's help I shouldn't have got them out of the field. As it was they waltzed from one end of the yard to the other like a fairground merry-go-round that had spun off its moorings, taking not a blind bit of notice of me. How I fastened up that welter of bodies I don't know, but I then phoned the Milk Marketing Board for A.I.

Back in the cowhouse milking was murder. Bluebell stood right up forward so that there was hardly room for me to crouch between her and the wall, rested her chin on the partition and gazed soulfully at the other two. All three of them were afflicted with St Vitus's dance and held back their milk to the best of their very considerable ability. Then when at last I submitted, with the grudging dispensation of three whole cows in one two-gallon pail, Rosie, first, hopped suddenly backwards into the dung channel with a jar that rattled my teeth, then took an enormous stride up again and placed her stupid, mucky hoof squarely into the bucket.

At that unpropitious moment a car horn blaring in the yard announced the arrival of the man with the A.I. Leaving the milk to run down the gutter I rescued the bent bucket and went out to meet him, smoothing my ruffled feathers. 'Hello,' I said, 'you've been quick and aren't I glad.' I treated him to a graphic description of the cows' behaviour and my own derring-do.

He grinned. 'First call,' he explained. He produced his certificate book. 'Two firsts and a repeat?' he confirmed, filling in the necessary forms. He donned his overalls — green to match his rubber boots. I made a mental note to buy myself some smart green wellies, such is the pinnacle of natty dressing down on the farm.

Pleasant fellows, the A.I. men, and on the way to the cowhouse we chatted harmoniously about how we preferred the early morning. 'Got a nice fresh feeling, like,' said the man appreciatively sniffing the breeze wafting past the honeysuckle. 'Oh, I agree,' I said earnestly, 'everything *is* fresh and *clean,* somehow.' And we opened the cowhouse door to find that Bluebell had gummed that one up too.

A heavy iron chain had as much restraining influence as cobweb when Bluebell took the urge to be off. Now it lay in a heap on the otherwise deserted floor of Bluebell's standing while Madam herself cavorted skittishly about in the grip stirring up an unsavoury soup of milk and manure which considerably reduced the wholesomeness of the morning.

What I thought about Bluebell then no words can express. Not that mere words would have had any effect. In fact nothing I or the A.I. man *did* had any effect, either. Blue was on a jag and determined to live it up with her friends. The three of us polka'd about in the mess in the confined area with Bluebell, beyond doubt, the dominating partner. Even the A.I. man gave up when Blue committed the unpardonable faux pas of making advances to *him.* She was served at length where she chose to anchor, tightly berthed between Rosie and Rhoda, and afterwards was forcibly banished to the back field. Usually, for an hour or so after service, we keep the cows quietly inside but on this occasion, Bluebell, in the mood she was in, said the A.I. man grimly, might be a bit of a problem. We were unanimous on that.

The A.I. man gunned his car up our steep cart-track, thankful that having at one go dealt with our entire herd he might reasonably expect to have seen the last of us for a whole year. (He was counting his chickens there, I'm afraid. Three weeks later when Blue came roaring into season again he drove straight onto the cart-track which, making good the wear and tear accidentally caused by their machines, the Waterboard men were just covering with a coat of quick drying cement ....)

Bluebell bawled imprecations after him until he vanished over the hill after which she bawled them at me. The two inside the cowhouse shouted back until the tiles lifted up and down like gills and the reverberations bounced the length of the valley.

Carrying my empty bucket towards the house I found another alarming incident getting into its stride. Mother and the Wards were gathered in a slightly agitated group around Roger who was sitting, apparently unconcernedly, on the paving.

'There's something wrong with him,' said mother anxiously. 'He walked outside all right but now he can't stand up!'

Kath had taken off Roger's shoes and was shaking them and feeling inside with her finger. 'I thought there might be a stone or something in them,' she said in her calm quiet voice as she worked the shoes back on Roger's feet and fastened the straps. 'Now then, Roger. Oops a daisy.'

Mother's concern seemed well-founded when, as Kath withdrew her support, Roger subsided suddenly to the paving again.

'It must be something in his sock,' I said. But it wasn't.

'He's been doing that all the time,' said Janet.

'He's pretending,' said David with six-year-old authority.

But it wasn't that either. There was no question about it, Roger had lost the use of his legs.

We eyed each other silently, the signal 'polio' transmitting wordlessly around the circle. My cow-battered mind was lurching about helplessly. That the doctor was needed was obvious but just how to manage that, wasn't. Doctor Scott lived over the moor in another village, and the surgery in our village, being little more than a whistle stop, did not run to a telephone. Gordon and the car were thirty miles away and at that time, the Wards had no transport of their own. We could have walked the two miles, taking it in turns to carry Roger but not in the fifteen minutes which was all that remained of surgery hours.

Then, right on cue, the Navy steamed in. Binnie, casually dropping in, she believed, for coffee but in reality reacting to trouble in that uncanny way she had of turning up with the goods just at the crucial moment, sized up the situation and bundled Roger and me off to the surgery in her car.

Now it was a funny thing about Binnie and ourselves. There seemed to be a strange sort of telepathic communication between us. Mother and I had only to muse about how we could do with a good cupboard in the back hall so we could stop trying to push utilitarian objects out of sight in corners, and Binnie would phone from her other home far away in the vicinity of Gordon's place of employment, and say her aunt wanted rid of a rather nice sideboard, and if it would be of any use to us she would drop it off for Gordon to bring home. We only had to be gathering up the sherds of our last useful-sized milk jug when Binnie would walk in with *three* which she had bought at a sale along with the brass oil lamp for which she had been bidding. The range of items she turned up with when we had been merely *thinking* about them was all embracing, from a winter play coat for Roger to a pair of wrought iron gates for the garden. It was quite uncanny, and one day when I had some new curtains to hang, being in a frivolous mood I said aloud to an empty room. 'Binnie, I could do with another brass curtain rod!' And when Gordon came home that night and said, Binnie had sent me some brass curtain rail. Could I do with it? I felt as if I'd been clubbed with a shillelagh. The fact that it was *rail* which needed runners and not *rod* for curtain rings made little difference. After all, no one's perfect. But I've guarded my thoughts ever since. It is too much like actually asking.

I was jolly glad that the magic was working that morning, however, and she whisked us to the doctor's minutes before the end of surgery. To our utter relief it wasn't polio, and we were sent on our way with medicine and the assurance that Roger would be better in a day or two. Outside we met a friend who told us that the same thing had happened to a little boy she knew. He had been back to normal in three days.

Normal everything was when we arrived back home too. There were Denis and Janet with stout sticks and grim expressions patrolling one side of the back field fence while Bluebell rampaged up and down at the other still hell bent on breaking through to the cowhouse. She'd done it once, said Denis admiringly. Smashed clean through the fence, and he'd patched up the gap with a sheet of corrugated iron.

The hullabaloo, we couldn't fail to notice, was now supplemented by sympathetic noises from the calves and Jess, reacting in her usual manner to their bellows, was howling like a couple of banshees. Later when I apologised for the day-long pandemonium to Mr Perry, a nice quiet man who with his family was occupying the bungalow that week, he smiled shyly and said very politely, Yes, Bluebell had been a little talkative, hadn't she? That, we said, was the understatement of the century.

14 Mellow fruitlessness

With the termination of school holidays summer made a sudden transition into autumn. The Wards returned home to recuperate and gather strength for next year, and although the bungalow would be occupied for a week or two yet, we began to think about and prepare for the winter which lay ahead. Not all that far ahead either, if September's weather was anything to go by, for the first half of the month was miserably cold and wet.

About this time our yearly load of straw was delivered, unloaded and stacked on the wide grass verge outside the Browns' house. As usual Gordon fumed at the inconvenience. He would have some other arrangement for this next year, see if he didn't, he said. He was to continue to say it, with variations, for years. However, that September, a beginning was made towards reform when, for the first time ever, the whole lot of it was led down to the farmyard that first evening. He was blowed, said Gordon, if he was going through another winter sledging down bales in penny numbers, and he shackled the sledge to the tractor forthwith. The Browns turned out in force to help, no doubt overcome with joy because their window wouldn't look out straight on to a wall of straw for the next six months, as it had on previous occasions.

Spurred on by all this willing assistance we worked like slaves, dismantling the main stack and building miniature ones on the sledge. Owing to the steepness and unevenness of the track and the added hindrance of overhanging trees we dare not load more than a score of bales at one time, though once we did risk a few more and the whole lot toppled over and entered the beck like a waterchute. We got unpleasantly wet hauling it out at top speed before the water could penetrate the bales. There were, it seemed, millions of bales and loading went on until well after dark.

Led by Steven carrying a lighted pressure lamp the procession turned out of the Browns' inlet and moved impressively down the road to our top gate. The tractor, with Gordon sitting regally upon it graciously dispensing Queen Mother-type waves right and left, came next. Behind it, in close attendance on the sledge, stumbled Binnie and myself, giving a hefty shove to the bales when necessary, closely followed by young Richard Brown who was stoutly carrying a bonus bale. Robert brought up the rear carrying a red paper-covered torch in lieu of a rear light. With the shrieking and screaming of sledge runners on cobbles, the cacophony created by the ancient tractor's proclivity to back-firing, volleys of glowing sparks exploding from the upright exhaust pipe and spraying everything within three yards' radius, the hiss and glare of the Tilley, and the red torch flashing in all directions like a neon sign, the whole cavalcade could have been mistaken for a reissue of Dante's Inferno.

We were nearly on our knees by the time the last load was led and the stack reassembled and roughly roofed with corrugated sheeting to deflect the rain, but we could go to bed thankful that it was a job well done.

Though not yet, we couldn't. Borne on the still night air, in the startling silence following the cutting out of the tractor's engine, three resentful voices reminded us accusingly, that we had forgotten to put them out, hadn't we? And when a few minutes later we remedied this and the cows stalked crossly into the back field they became even huffier than before. Someone, they yelled, had stuck a whopping great strawstack in it.

Still we hadn't finished with that straw. On the following Saturday Gordon and I shifted it again, cramming bales into every available building. The hay in the barn had settled down by then, and the space in the apex of the barn roof absorbed most of the bales. At last the straw was protected from the weather — and from the cows, who having got over the horrors induced by its existence, went to the other extreme and wouldn't leave it alone, playfully working bales loose with their heads and scattering the stuff about until the vicinity of the stack looked as if it had been laid with coconut matting.

Did I realise, said Gordon, that that was the third time we had handled the straw already?

I did realise it. I realised it with every muscle I possessed and I knew that when I came to be strewing it around for winter bedding I should recognise as old acquaintances every individual wisp. All four and a half tons of it.

The following afternoon was devoted to fruit picking. If it hadn't been for the wasps the whole thing could have been wound up in a couple of hours because the crop, as in the previous two seasons, was not a good one. Indeed, the first season had been utterly disastrous, the entire harvest comprising seven raspberries and half a plum wrested from a thieving blackbird. I had made a rather skimpy pudding with those. We each got a raspberry but I forgot who drew the plum. Since that year the only really reliable fruiter has been the Keswick growing behind the cowhouse where an unending supply of manure ensures a well nourished tree.

Not that the others can be blamed too much. At an age well over the century mark, many of them must be feeling past it, though given the right conditions they can still produce valiantly, and in our eleven years of ownership have twice surprised us with an outstandingly bumper crop. According to the notes sensibly recorded by their planter long ago, there were three dozen different varieties of apple and a dozen of plum as well as a number of pears and cherries. I wish I could identify the survivors. I should be honoured to make the acquaintance of Royal George and the Glory of York and I am certain that Walter Blacket and Tom Suggett are worthy, upstanding characters. I'm not so sure about Rock Head and Leathercoat. There's a touch of Chicago in the twenties there, I fancy; an aura of snap brims and shoulder holsters. I should feel more at home with Bessie Harrison. Can't you see her, standing on the doorstep in her starched white apron talking to Lawrence who, I see by the notes, is a plum?

Gordon finds all insects and affiliated creatures utterly fascinating and will expound on the life cycle of a tick at the drop of a hat. He would have been a dedicated bee keeper if he hadn't discovered, while helping Westwath's former owner with his, that he was allergic to their stings. Balked of that ambition Gordon switched his admiration to vespa vulgaris, the common wasp. Not that he *kept* them, of course, but he did nothing to discourage them either.

Up to that time I hadn't taken a good look at a wasps' nest, but Gordon soon put that right, and I had to admit that they were beautifully constructed — in shape something like a smoothed off Jerusalem artichoke. Needless to say, the ones I examined were uninhabited. They were silver grey in colour and made from our chewed up garage door. Chivvied by Gordon, I watched them at work on it, scraping the wood away with a surprisingly loud scratching sound. The expression on Gordon's face was respectful in the extreme. You would have thought that our wasps had been awarded a Nobel Prize for science. The garage door fell off in the end but Gordon said that was the fault of the hinges.

The wasps tilted on their pedestal a fraction when Gordon found they were repaying his kindness by raiding the plums, and that, what on the surface appeared to be plump luscious fruit, turned out to be skin stuffed with drunken roisterers. A ladder thrust into the branches dislodged dozens more which showered over us like fur-coated raindrops, and I retired to the house to what I mistakenly thought was safety. Mistaken, because it transpired I had a stowaway inside my blouse. It thrust a needle agonisingly into my diaphragm and with sudden startling illumination revealed that I was allergic to wasps. It was hours before the pile-driver that had been my heart stopped thumping, and I could breathe normally again. But, although Gordon had had a very worried afternoon, he still retained more than a modicum of sympathy for the wasp. I must have squashed it, he said defensively.

Short on jam and bottled fruit we may have been but that was hardly the case with firewood, thanks to Gordon's chainsaw and my cold chisels and seven pound hammer.

I don't know if log splitting is an art or a science but either way I am confident I could pass A levels in it. Many of the logs — for instance, those from that elm tree pulled out of the beck — were as much as a yard across and knobbly as all get out, but with a practical eye I sought out the fine medulary lines, poised on them the wide cold chisel (holding it unflinchingly with my left hand) and swung the seven pound lump of cast steel down on it with the other. Round the log I would go as if slicing a cake and the pile of sections at my feet would grow most satisfactorily.

Sometimes an extra tough one gave trouble and the chisel either bounced off and got lost in the debris of chippings and bark pieces or jammed in the log. Then I would try to free it by forcing in another alongside and get that stuck too, and when the log was sprouting as many fins as a John Dory I would have to admit defeat and wait for Gordon to come home and untangle it.

Late on the evening of October thirty-first I was still splitting logs. Sitting beneath the enormous beech that grows by the wath. Antony was at a party, and I was sitting there with a storm lantern to light his way across the beck when he returned. The light threw into relief the soaring smooth grey limbs of the tree. Lines, which when translated into stone command respect and awe in cathedrals throughout Christendom. I could hardly tear away my eyes from the sight and felt a certain sympathy with our tree-worshipping ancestors. There are few trees which fail to have this effect on me and because of the sylvan quality of Westwath I live in an almost permanent state of bemusement — though Gordon says unkindly, that I shouldn't be noticeably different in the Sahara.

15 Tree talk

One day, when I find time, I shall make an inventory of the trees at Westwath. One Christmas I did count the hollies, got to the forty mark and gave up, uncertain whether or not to include the babies that grew barely taller than my knee.

Poor and sandy though the soil is, it supports two majestic beeches; the second one grows rather too close to the house and in summer, the sun imperfectly penetrating the canopy of leaves, imparts a greenish light to the rooms so that we have a sensation of living beneath the sea. But its proximity gives us one enormous advantage, an opportunity to observe at close quarters its response to the changing seasons. For six months of the year we study — with, I confess, growing boredom — the grace of intricately laced branches, until suddenly, in early May the long slender grey buds blush to a delicate pink, ethereally lovely when spotlighted by the sun against a purple backcloth of thundercloud.

That shaft of sun and May thundercloud backdrop are the perfect props on our Westwath stage. The livid sky behind grey-tufted rowans and apple, or spattered with palest green bird cherry, is chiaroscuro an artist would give his right hand to have created, but the supreme glory — the highlight of my year — is reached in mid-month with the explosion of the double white flowering cherry. The whole thing — and it must be all of thirty feet tall — appears to have been dunked in white emulsion paint, so completely do the pristine flowers hide the leaves and branches, and what the dark thundercloud can do with that is nothing short of a spiritual experience. I give thanks for it every year.

From then on the purple background is superfluous. We can enjoy the myriad white spikes of bird cherry (*prunus padus*, if you are a clever-clogs like me who has all the Sunday names off pat) just as well without it. Its scent is heavy and some say sickly, but is a basic ingredient of the perfume of the month. The month might be May, but in this part of the world the hawthorn's common name would more aptly be June flower, for it is then we enjoy it. The hitherto pendant beech leaves have already lifted and spread to the horizontal and are deepening in hue when the tardy oaks and ashes venture to enlarge their buds. I don't blame them. Delicate bunches of ash leaves are regularly reduced to shreds of black rag, even in late June, in this decidedly severe frost pocket.

The oaks will not be hurried. There is nothing rash about an oak. Not for them the undisciplined restlessness of the hazels, say, who send up tall new wands in a season, only to be cut back and coppiced in a year or two. The oak is a deliberate patient genus, as dependable as the wooden ships it sent to defeat the Armada. At the gate to the wood a patriarchal giant stands guard. Its hefty, black, far spreading arms holding back the exuberant younger, giddier generation in its flamboyant late spring clothing, like a lone sane policeman at a pop star's wedding. For all its cautious welcoming of the year it makes up for it at the other end when, still green and virile, it looks down its nose at its sere and yellow companions. And the only moral of that, that I can think of, is those who stay in bed until midday don't fall asleep in their suppers.

Only slightly earlier risers are the alders. Goodness knows how many of those stand peering into the beck like silent watchful fishermen; certainly too many to count. Most of them are multiple trunked with gnarled nether limbs veining the river banks. Between these exposed roots are dark caverns and little sandy beaches where water voles and moorhens lead busy private lives. The moorhens are shy and make off in a volley of ringing alarm notes but the voles entertain us for hours — pottering in and out of the little coves and swimming in arrowheads of ruffled water to another shore, perhaps pausing en route, where the bird cherry dips low, to balance on a waterborne twig and munch a leaf.

Sunlight refracting from the water projects an opalescence on the tree trunks which seems to float upwards in a perpetual motion that sends me into a trance. Ash trees dip elegant fingers to the water and casually pick out sparkling gems. There is enough going on by the river bank to last anyone a lifetime. Surprisingly no willows grow by the beck although across the road in the top field a goat willow yields an armful of fluffy, fat catkins to delight us around Eastertime. A vase of these intermixed with slender hazel and red-brown alder catkins is a promising reminder that spring is only around the corner.

Touching wood and muttering incantations I hereby put on record that the dreaded Dutch elm disease has not yet laid its destructive hand on our trees, and English elms and wych elms grow to imposing heights, neck and neck with the farmyard's old larches. Half a dozen heavy headed horsechestnut trees ensure a lavish supply of conkers, more, even, than the children can cope with. They lie neglected on the ground and put up green umbrellas the following spring.

The wide, spreading branches of one chestnut were requisitioned by the boys who saw in them a desirable building site. The resulting treehouse constructed from timber, corrugated iron and plastic sheeting looked like the consequence of a head on collision between an Emmett train and a dirigible, but the architects saw it as an improvement on Compton Wynyates or the Taj Mahal. It was a relief when the leaves grew and softened the outline.

At reproduction our chestnuts and sycamores beat rabbits. So does the poplar whose suckers would bristle over half an acre if we didn't scythe them to the ground each spring. If we turned our backs for a fortnight the jungle would be let in at Westwath.

All this arborescence and yet I haven't touched on the birches whose mottled black and silver trunks spring self-consciously from a wash of slender-necked harebells. Those edging the Scar field and surmounting the steep rocky face of the ravine are old, gnarled and full of witch growths like knots in a tangled head of hair. Nor have I mentioned the solitary old walnut whose narrow trunk, drawn upwards to the light, hovers in a state of irresolute disequilibrium, produces no nuts but houses a brood of starlings every spring.

The walnut is slowly suffocating in the wide spreading skirts of a yew whose pyramidical shape and enormous size would not disgrace an arboretum. It is the remaining one of a pair. Its twin had to go when its black-green flounces overlaid the house and inflicted perpetual twilight on the dining room. The newly cut wood of the yew was a revelation. It was the warm glowing colour of sun ripened apricots. Even now, years later, the wide table-like stump is pleasant to look at. The original colour has faded but the peeling bark reveals a sort of undergarment hanging in folds of shimmering oyster silk. It is said that the great gardener and plantsman, A. E. Bowles so admired his yew trees that he regularly scrubbed their trunks with soap and water.

Westwath even boasts an exotic. A tall, symmetrical, monkey puzzle tree. There was a time when *we* didn't care for them, either, lumping them together with other Victorian monstrosities. But that was before we owned one or had taken the trouble to study one. Now we appreciate the delicately detailed fashioning. Regular, spiky, spiney leaves thickly wrap the swooping branches which lead the eye smoothly upwards to the summit where, some years, perch green cones, big and round as footballs. Even the trunk is beautiful; a model of meticulous design which is displayed to perfection when snow clings to the raised pattern. It looks like an elongated pineapple. Like most evergreens it sheds its leaves unobtrusively in summer. Unobtrusively, that is, to non-gardeners. The rest of us notice all right for the monkey puzzle, like the holly, has a heinous vice. Try weeding beneath it. For extreme masochism it has the edge on the hair shirt.

16 Stonecrop

When I told Binnie, that while I was splitting logs beneath the beech, it had suddenly dawned on me that it was Hallowe'en, the night of the witches, she laughed me to scorn. I must be daft, she said, if I thought any sensible witch would venture near Westwath. She'd be roped in to do some work.

A touch of bitterness there, perhaps? But Binnie had no one to blame but herself. It had been entirely her own idea that we should cut and gather bracken for the cows' winter bedding.

Situated on the edge of the moor itself, Binnie's house was lapped by waves of bracken, tall, lush and green in summer but turning russet and ragged now in late autumn. Neighbouring farmers had already cut large swathes out of the moor and were leading heaped trailers away to their stackyards.

Our work force consisted of Binnie and her daughter

Judith, Robert, Antony and myself. Binnie and I because we were older and, what was more influential, bigger, commandeered the saw-edged sickles and plunged into the thick fronds. They grew like a wall, chest high and dense. We scooped them into our left arms, sliced at them with our hooks and left them in heaps for the labourers to gather up. The labourers followed on our heels with large sacks and bigger complaints. Bracken, they said, scratched and tickled. It was full of midges that bit. It made them hot and sticky and it was their turn to have the sickles. Five minutes after we had started they said the sacks were full, and after Binnie and I had rammed down the contents to prove that they weren't, the children said they were thirsty and why couldn't they have the sickles?

We moved slowly up the hillside, 'The Reapers' brought to life.

Robert loaded his full sack onto the wheelbarrow which he had, with considerable effort, dragged up from the farmyard, and careered off downhill with it. We others, less wiry, heaved our sacks into Binnie's car, piled ourselves on top and drove down to the garage. From there we lugged them across the field to the farmyard and tipped them into a disused calf pen. Released from the sacking the bracken expanded like soapsuds, filled the pen up to the roof and foamed out of the doorway. It looked satisfyingly plenteous and Antony, feeling that enough was enough, vanished for the rest of the afternoon. The rest of us sweated on and jammed two more carloads into the calf pen before calling it a day.

That evening we learned that Gordon had also had bedding in mind. He came home with the Morris Traveller bursting at the seams with sacks of soft wood shavings, free for the collecting, from a Teesside wood yard.

The cows' winter comfort was ensured which only goes to show how preferable is the lot of an animal to that of a human at Westwath.

I ought not to complain. Even amid the constant round of chores I found time to indulge in my favourite hobby; marvelling nevertheless at destiny's lopsided way of doing things. Wouldn't you have thought that with a lifestyle like mine, nature would have compensated by endowing me with a spare time interest like stamp collecting or doing card tricks? But no, it saddled me with an all-consuming passion for gardening. Not the dainty stuff like dead-heading the roses either, but muscle punishing things such as digging pools, raising walls and creating paths and paving, all entailing involvement with great lumps of sandstone.

Back in Hull — a stoneless district — we bought a ton of broken paving slabs from the City Council. Normally a ton doesn't go very far but ours hardly ever stopped travelling. We couldn't afford any more so I made that one load do the work of a dozen. I began with a low wall, a path and a patio. Then I took up the path and laid a terrace. Later I shifted the terrace and made a rock garden with steps, which was quite a feat in a completely flat area, and all the time I yearned for more stone.

When we moved to Westwath I felt like the storybook child who finds everything made of chocolate and candy. My mouth watered at the sight of all the natural rock beckoning from all directions.

The house is built of it; huge blocks of sandstone dressed square at the edges and set so closely on top of one another that mortar is hardly discernible. The surface is irregular so that snow clings to it in winter and in summer oblique rays from the evening sun throw over it a pattern of shadows. Its colours are warm, ranging through every hue from oatmeal, via cinder-toffee to the deepest shade of caramel, yet in some lights it has a blue cast and after rain something else again. From the chisel marks of long dead masons to the fossilised skeletons of even longer defunct crustaceans there is always something to read on its surface. And you can't say that about modern brick.

Stone boundary walls, wide and ancient, were already there and stone steps led from the garden up to the hayfield. Tall gateposts, broad and strong enough to support lock-gates, stood at the entrance to each field, and in the farmyard four other posts standing at the corners of a rectangle marked the site of an old sawpit. The grindstone set in its own stone trough bore witness to its years of use. I would have given my eyebrows to have had that in my other garden but it would have been incongruously out of its element there. And then there were the bee stones. A number of people have offered more than their eyebrows for those, their covetousness intensifying if anything, when they learned that they were not, as they had presumed, staddle stones. Bee stones are flat topped and petal shaped, standing on a stalk, mushroom-fashion, and were plinths for the old straw bee skeps.

The only drawback to all this bounty was that underground, rock lay only a few inches beneath the soil which didn't help Gordon's temper when he was trying to let in new fence posts. Or mine, for that matter, when I was digging new flower beds. I prized out the stones, replacing them with compost, and used them to construct a terrace. Our former Hull neighbour called while this was going on and said she wasn't surprised a bit. Binnie was more scathing. 'It's a good thing you don't live near Stonehenge,' she said. 'They would have to tie it down or you'd shift that lot, as well.'

I shouldn't. I should just plant it up with aubrieta.

17 A mad whirl in town

Gordon was away at work each weekday but I seldom left the farm so when Mother decided to stay with my cousin in York for a couple of weeks and we were to drive her there on the following Saturday, I was delighted. York, where something of interest is to be seen around every corner, is my favourite city and I looked forward to a little culture coupled with a bit of Christmas shopping. Excitedly, I ran to earth the shopping list headed, 'York'. The shopping list was tatty, dog-eared and long past its first youth. It had been launched in spring when hope springs eternal and we optimistically anticipated a day in town to shop for commodities unobtainable locally — exotic things like brass handles for cabinets and piping cord for loose covers. Items such as bedding plants, inflatable armbands for non-swimmers and bathing trunks (Antony) were, as the year progressed, being pushed off the page by pullover (Robert), and gloves (everybody). I crossed off near the top, sandles (me), and wrote at the bottom, Christmas presents.

It was nearly 11 am as we passed Fylingdales Early Warning Station after wrenching ourselves away from our demanding smallholding. All the animals had been given extra rations to see them through the day. Water troughs had been filled and filled again as the contrary creatures insisted — would we believe it? — they were parched that morning. Charlotte was locked inside the house with milk, meat and earthbox, and last of all, Jess was clipped to her chain and blandished with the juiciest bone from her week's supply. We did that with a lot of jolly head tousling which didn't fool her one bit. She had known instinctively from the moment we opened the doghouse door that we were going out, was pretty sure that our plans did not include her, and so contrived to put herself in a dozen different places at once. Wherever we went we stumbled over a dejected dog looking more heart-wrenching than the little match girl and the whole of Uncle Tom's Cabin put together.

The afternoon began all right, although a little behind schedule after depositing mother and young Roger at Marian's house and finding a car park with a vacant lot. To allow me the opportunity to race through the shops without the impedimenta of my nearest and dearest Gordon said he would take the boys to the Castle Museum. We agreed to meet at the car park at 4.30 pm to allow enough time to go to Marian's for tea and pick up Roger before returning home for evening milking.

The trouble with York is that it is so distracting, and the temptation to spend as much time gazing at the outside architecture of the medieval shops as the inside merchandise, accounted for much of the incredibly swift passage of time. Nevertheless, it was with three overfull shopping bags that, on the stroke of 4.30, I tottered in the direction of the car park. Cinderella probably had the same sense of urgency as she made for *her* coach.

The car park was full but our white topped Traveller was easy to spot, and gladly I dumped the heavy bags beside it. I balanced on top of them a large white paper bag containing a pair of jeans for Gordon and draped myself gratefully over the car bonnet. A woman climbed into a neighbouring car and sank into the driving seat. 'My feet are killing me!' she called cheerfully, gave me a friendly nod and drove out of the compound. My own feet, I realised, were equally homicidal but as I hadn't a key to the car I could only lean heavily upon it and wonder what fathead had designed away the old running-boards. At 5 pm, lamenting a wasted half hour which could have been more profitably and comfortably spent in a nice warm shop, I picked up the heavy bags, tucked the jeans under my arm and walked to the road corner, battling against the current of returning car owners and feeling thoroughly annoyed. None of my family was to be seen in any direction though I stood there for ages rehearsing what I would say to them when they came. It was draughty on the corner so I walked back to the car and rehearsed something more telling.

Blank spaces were spreading about me as doors slammed, engines started and vehicles moved towards the exits where bars busily semaphoring up and down ejected them into anonymity. After a while, apart from a sort of caravan converted from a bus which was parked, apparently permanently, right at the back, our car was the only one left.

I occupied fifteen bitter minutes watching the people in the brightly lighted camping bus enjoying a meal, then I counted the windowpanes in the nearby hospital. When that palled I walked over to the river, bags and all, and stared moodily into its murky depths until I got morbid and imagined I could see three corpses floating in it. Because by six o'clock I was getting very worried. Good heavens, by that time we ought to have left Marian's and started the homeward run.

I went back to the car and counted the hospital windowpanes again. All of them this time, including the ones partly obscured by trees and a wall, which I had ignored before. Then I did a re-count and came up with a different answer which I immediately forgot because my heart wasn't really in it. It is not easy to think positively about fenestration when one's family has mysteriously disappeared. I knew, now, exactly how Jean Simmons felt in 'So Long at the Fair' when her brother vanished from the Paris hotel. But she, lucky thing, had Dirk Bogarde to console her and my chances of that I guessed to be slim.

Those blasted bus people were having another cup of something. My stomach was an empty void. I had already churned the contents of all three bags into the semblence of a well-used lucky dip in search of something edible and come up with a packet of chocolate rolls that were so well sealed in plastic that I couldn't get into them. I had attacked the thing from all directions, even going so far as to stab at it frenziedly with a hairgrip. Unfortunately it was the cushion-ended type which merely skidded across the surface like a slate pencil and shot off to be lost for ever in the welter of items in the largest bag.

I glared malevolently at the bus and willed someone to offer me a cup of tea. They *knew* I had been waiting there in the deserted car park for the last two hours. They could hardly have missed seeing me wilting there like a lone palm tree in the middle of the Sahara, but never threw me so much as a glance of sympathy. *I* couldn't be like that, I thought bitterly, to anyone in that predicament. (And as a matter of fact I did come across someone in a similar situation only this week. I couldn't offer tea or a comfortable chair so I told her what I'm telling you instead. It didn't seem to cheer her as much as I had expected.)

Then, at seven o'clock, just when I had made up my mind to go and phone the police and ask if a man and two children had recently been admitted to hospital stroke morgue, or if not, would they mind getting the museum caretaker to search the place in case they had been locked in the padded cell or somewhere, and if they hadn't, to kindly see that they *were* ... I beheld coming towards me across the acres of concrete, three hurrying figures.

I managed not to raise my voice much above a scream as I asked the obvious question, but when I perceived that Gordon's expression was that of a man who had suffered and was reaching the end of his tether I concluded my remarks and threw the subject open to general discussion.

They *had* overrun their time a little, Gordon admitted. *But* — I had opened my mouth to endorse this — the trouble was, he and Robert had been deeply engrossed in the museum's treasures when they discovered that they had lost Antony. Really lost him. He simply wasn't *there*.

Immediately he had my sympathy. It figured. Antony was the type of child things happened to.

At two years old he had been spotted by our neighbour up a ladder that Gordon had left leaning against the wall by the upstairs bathroom window. Antony, said Margery weakly, was standing about sixteen rungs up. Backwards. Facing outwards, and she hadn't dared to speak to him in case he stepped off. She had good reason for her fears. He had already stepped into space from the top of the staircase and been caught, a fraction above ground level, by Gordon who just happened to be passing. This time he was rescued by Gordon going up the ladder while I held Antony's attention through the bathroom window. We had a cup of coffee afterwards to settle our nerves, Antony drinking his from the plastic beaker he had been allotted after having twice bitten pieces out of glass ones.

Antony's head has been stitched so often it looks like a sampler. It has been stitched in Hull, Leeds and Whitby. The day after the Leeds operation he walked into the corner of our friends' house where we were staying, and gashed his head on the other side. Considerably shaken, Margaret and I cut away the hair and stuck the wound together with Elastoplast. We couldn't face another hospital visit like the last one when, because the stitches had been put in badly and had to be re-done, the entire casualty ward was embroiled as if for some major calamity.

When, celebrating our wedding anniversary for once, Gordon and I aspired to an evening's run out to the sea — taking the boys with us because we wouldn't have inflicted Antony on our worst enemy — guess who fell, fully dressed, off a breakwater into the sea?

When at five years old he started school, I collapsed with relief. My vigilance relieved by his teacher, I could attend, now, to other things. Guess who again, out of all the children of that admittance class who conscientiously planted peas in blotting paper, was the one who carefully wedged his up his nostril and had, on only his second day at school, to be driven home by the school caretaker in the headmistress's car?

Anyone, then, capable of this and much, much more, would find losing himself in a museum elementary stuff.

A fortnight after that well remembered day — Time being the great healer — I had almost forgotten the experience and was looking forward to our next York visit when we were to collect mother from Marian's civilised home and bring her back to ours.

We arose extra early on Saturday morning. Gordon went out to milk the cows and feed the stock while I gave the house an extra going over. Mother's idea of tidiness was less elastic than mine and would have been further strengthened by elegant city living, so spit and polish was the order of the day. Working at top speed I made the place presentable, packed sandwiches and a flask of coffee, changed out of working clothes, dressed the boys in their best and then Gordon came in with the milk.

The day before we had had to call in the vet to all six calves who had unaccountably picked up some germ and were scouring badly. Water and glucose for three days, said Mr Burn. What about milk? we had asked. Definitely no milk, said the vet.

What we were going to do with six gallons of milk — even with our capacity for the stuff — we couldn't imagine. A pig-keeping neighbour refused it regretfully on the grounds that the pigs' stomachs weren't used to it and the sudden change might set them scouring too ....

Actually we got rid of it all very suddenly. One second, three brimming bucketfuls plus one currently in use three pint jug were lined up on the kitchen table. The next, Antony had leaned his weight on the rather top-heavy extended table leaf and the whole lot went over like Niagara.

One brief moment of silent shock and I gave up trying to remember why a Britisher always keeps her cool. I ran out into the garden and threw myself into a wonderful orgy of simple, down-to-earth, screaming hysterics.

18   MRCVS

Compared with the last one, winter was easy although roads were frequently so impassable that the children were unable to go to school. On these days snowmen erupted like mushrooms and the Rayburn was perpetually steaming with drying gloves and boots. The familiar deep throb of the snowplough, scraping shovels and voices carrying on the frosty air as people heaped grit beneath ineffectual wheels, were background noises accompanying our daily routine. Again the Scar's architecture was perpendicular with icicles, a Wookey Hole in glass.

And once more, Westwath's delicate internal organs flared up.

Mind you, a change is as good as a rest, they say, and we hadn't had trouble with the drains before — at least not uncomfortably so. The first I knew about it was one washday when I pulled out the plug to empty the sink and it returned to me a thousandfold. Flooding over me with the soapy water came a re-experience of the sensations I had felt over the business of Bluebell's cleansing and this carry-on, I instinctively felt, was going to be worse. It was.

The removal of the cover over the inspection chamber of

the septic tank revealed a sight I hope never to see again. The only way I could tackle the job was to switch off my brain, turn myself into an automaton and with the aid of the wheelbarrow and my Happy Mother's Day present transfer its contents to the farthest side of the midden. Gordon came home as I was scraping the bottom, blanched, decided he didn't want any tea, and with set face went in search of the chimney cleaning rods. I didn't fancy tea either, despite having had no lunch and the two of us rodded the pipe, swilled and swept once more, feeling that we should never be clean again.

Eventually everything *was* clean and functioning normally, continuing to do so until years later when my first book was published. On the very morning that our home-town newspaper's Women's Page reporter came to do a feature on me, Fate and the drains rose up against us again, and to his mortification Gordon was photographed filthy and festooned in hose-pipe.

The calves had grown into hefty animals now — apart from Totty who still had a lot of ground to make up — and had developed their own idiosyncrasies. Bruno had two. As well as forever walking about with an empty bucket on his head, saying he was the Black Prince, he had an overriding ambition to toss us into the next county. Rendered defenceless with my arms full of hay, I was his main target. As I walked across the field towards the hut where the hayrack was, he was right behind, bouncing my bottom with his head — luckily bucketless — so that either I bounced up and down with him at every step or I pounded over the hummocks to plunge headlong into the hayrack, depending what speed took his fancy.

Passing the calf field one day while Gordon was feeding up, I was interested to hear a series of bumps followed by yells of pain and rage — Bump — 'Ow. Geroff.' Bump — 'Ow. Geroff,' issuing from the hut. I dashed over to see what was up, and was in time to see Gordon stuffing hay into the rack and rhythmically banging his head on the corrugated iron roof with every jerk from Bruno.

He only did it because he liked us. He was a friendly

animal and always accompanied me affectionately whenever I went through his field.

I was so accustomed to being thrown about like a shuttlecock that when one morning I was allowed to carry in the hay unmolested I knew that something was amiss. Sure enough, Bruno was standing sadly beneath a blackthorn bush, with a running nose and all the bounce knocked out of him. He coughed once or twice as I stared at him. Donald, one of the bought-in calves, a black and white Friesian, was also looking peaky. Shivering too.

Without much difficulty I herded the pair into the hut, barricaded them inside at the back with a hurdle and went to search the medicine chest for something appropriate. I found a bottle of patent animal medicine which claimed to cure everything except decomposition. It smelt strongly of spices and was, it warned in red letters, poisonous to humans.

To dose a calf it is an advantage if you are equipped with three hands. One to hold back the head, another to open the mouth and the third to tip up the bottle. Handicapped with only two, I hung my weight around the neck of each beast in turn, backed him into a corner and dribbled the liquid down his throat — mostly inside. At midday I repeated the dose with even more success. I wondered what a brass plate with MRCVS after my name would look like on the farm gate. At evening feed time as I confidently strode forth carrying a bucket of milk in one hand, a bucket of cattle rearing nuts on which rested the medicine and dosing bottles in the other, and began evening surgery, it seemed that I only had to decide *which* of our two entrance gates I should hang it on and I should be in business.

The first thing that went wrong was that Agnes, a beautiful and powerful Angus heifer, cleaned up her own meal and ambled over to see what she was missing inside the hut. I had carefully placed the nuts and milk inside the doorway while I advanced on Donald, dose at the ready, and Agnes, thinking she had hit the jackpot at last, plunged her head into the milk.

That bucket was a nice, unbattered plastic one only used

for carrying milk to the troughs, so I made a grab for it. The movement startled Agnes. She backed sharply away giving the door such a whack with her rear that it lifted it clean off its pintle and socket-type hinges. Down it crashed inwards, flattening the hurdle fence.

Or it would have flattened it if Donald's head hadn't become ensnared between two of its cross-pieces. Wearing it like a ruff he blundered excitedly about, stood in the nuts, split open the plastic bucket, and — the crowning indignity which knocked me and my brass plate for six — played the old ladder joke, swinging around the end of the fence and bringing me a forceful thwack across the rear which sent me flying.

That calf hut was the setting for another of my peculiar adventures. At half past six one Sunday morning I was pushing hay into the rack when the light from the door was dimmed and a man's voice spoke behind me. I spun about, swallowing a yell. People just don't happen to be passing Westwath at that time of morning.

'Hullo,' said the man and stood looking at me.

'Hullo,' I said warily, and with that the conversation ground to a halt.

There was a long pause, then in an accent I couldn't place the man asked if we had a telephone? He asked with no sense of urgency but more as if he were merely making polite conversation. We had, I said, and wondered whether to offer him a bite of hay as an impasse appeared to have been reached. Then to my relief he stepped backwards out of the doorway. I quickly slipped outside, sidled past him and made off for home. He fell into step beside me still smiling pleasantly but saying nothing.

In a flash I knew what he was. An escaped convict. His next words confirmed it. Had I, he asked, seen anything of a helicopter?

And you know, I had! At least I'd heard it. It had been circling about for ages as if searching for someone.

Pull yourself together woman, I told myself as my knocking knees threatened to trip me up. Don't let him know you know. Say something to allay his suspicions.

Something ordinary and casual.

'Are you doing the Lyke Wake Walk?' I asked inspirationally.

The route of this now famous and well-trodden long distance walk across the moors passed within a mile of us and sometimes stragglers or droppers-out took short cuts across our land.

'Er, ye-es,' he said unconvincingly.

To show how unsuspicious I was I nonchalantly hummed a tune. Unfortunately I hit on a tricky bit from Rigoletto which was beyond my range and the next thing was, the man was looking oddly at *me*. What if this disquieting character were to knock me on the head and run off with the egg money? Gordon wasn't at the house but young Robert was.

'Keep your eye on that man,' I hissed. 'Try to hear who he's phoning while I go and get your father.'

When I came back with a bewildered husband in tow the man had gone. Robert took the wind out of my sails.

'It's all right, Mum. It's all *right*. He's not an escaped prisoner. He's on manoeuvres. He's just gone off in an army truck!'

I must have been one of the few people in Britain who were unaware of the extensive military manoeuvres involving half of Europe that were taking place that weekend.

I was so relieved. I counted the egg money. There was eight shillings and fourpence.

19 *Tip*

Charlotte Philippa Arthur Georgina was growing up and was, like all the other animals about the place, a creature to be reckoned with. Her colouring was arresting for a start. It was so unusual that walkers passing the gate were pulled back as if on elastic.

'That little cat is *pink* and *blue*,' said one little girl tugging at her mother's sleeve. And so she was. What in another cat might have been mottled ginger and grey was, in Charlotte, lightened to delicate pastel shades.

'Got a bit of Siamese in her, hasn't she?' was a comment we were to hear at intervals for years. A reference not only to Charlotte but also to her many descendants whenever the pink and blue appeared or a kinky tail or wedge-shaped face turned up. It may have been so though no one could recall a Siamese cat ever having been in the district.

'Kittens seem to *blow* about, don't they?' said Binnie. And indeed the pretty scrap of fluff appeared to have no more substance than the withered leaf it was batting about. At either end of a length of string Charlotte and Roger entertained each other for hours.

She amused me when I was digging the vegetable garden one day, by walking along the old top fence rail through the entire length of the thick holly hedge that had grown up around it. She climbed up the near end and shakily but determinedly commenced her long trek, appearing, at intervals, in the thinner parts trudging along like a feline Colonel Forster penetrating the forests of the Amazon. At other times she could be glimpsed ignominiously hanging on by her elbows, back legs scrabbling for a hold, ears back and a set expression on her face. Irritably she refused offers of help, airily informing me that she always did that at fenceposts. It was good for toning up the muscles. Not for one instant did she think of turning back but rustled on for the rest of the afternoon, emerging at length victorious and decorated with holly leaves in place of a laurel wreath.

Not only did she accompany me to the vegetable patch, she joined the growing procession that escorted me wherever I went. My retinue now consisted of Roger, Jess, Charlotte and Tip.

Tip was Jess's daughter. I haven't mentioned her before because she was very much a part of a sad episode in our lives, one which we don't like to think about even now.

Tip was one of a litter of six born to Jess two years earlier. She was short haired and the only plain-looking puppy out of the lot — the others had long thick wool like their mother and were beautiful — but she was the only bitch. We sold the boys and kept Tip because we believed that two dogs of the same sex would be less trouble in the long run.

It was fun having a puppy. At least we humans thought so. Jess wasn't so keen and usually contrived to have the garden gate between herself and her daughter, Jess lying unconcernedly on the garden side of it while Tip dashed boisterously up and down at the other.

Tip was a canine version of Antony — insouciant and accident-prone. Show her a hole and she would fall in it; a wall and she'd fall off it. In the absence of either hole or wall she fell over her own feet, and always leaped before she looked. Her first encounter with a horse landed her at the vet's having a broken thigh pinned together.

Broken leg notwithstanding, she still leaped obstacles with gay abandon while we cringed and yelped for her. Walks along the moor became quite lively affairs with Jess forgetting her middle-aged dignity, bearing out that extraordinary theorem that children keep you young.

And now the rabbits had to watch out. One day, to my horror, Tip caught one and the poor thing screamed out in terror.

'Drop it, Tip,' I called. 'Drop it!' I hardly expected her to obey thinking the temptation to kill would be too strong. But even though high with excitement, she released it, wistfully watching it bound away with great airborne leaps. The look she turned on me spoke volumes but I didn't care. I was only delighted with that further proof of her obedience.

Rabbiting, Tip decided, was to be her vocation, and dug holes all around the henhouse in case any were lurking there. Just when it was beginning to look archaeologically interesting — a moated, ramparted henhut is not met with every day — she abandoned that site and reconnoitred farther afield. This was a bit of a problem as roaming dogs are not welcome in sheep country. Almost invariably she was to be found at Stoney Flatt Foss excavating ditches and throwing up earthworks, chattering incessantly to the rabbits who, forewarned being forearmed, had made off for healthier climes. But after an occasion when she had been brought home on a piece of string from a neighbouring farm we felt our nerves would suffer less if her movements were restricted, and we threaded the loop of her lead over a long line that ran the length of the farmyard.

She complained about it, of course. She was turning into a tram, she wailed, as she galloped back and forth from one end to the other.

Jess lay smugly to one side of the tramline, just far enough away to be out of her daughter's reach. My sympathies were all with Tip as she made futile snaps in the direction of her mother's ears because Jess's expression was insufferable even to us.

Of course Tip still had her freedom on our walks, and in the evening she shared a rug in the kitchen with Jess. Tip and Charlotte had become great friends. Charlotte, growing up, had fallen in love with love, and in the absence of a boy friend, took her troubles every three weeks to Tip. At these times they would both sit on the orchard wall and talk about it until Tip fell off.

Charlotte never fell but was often pushed — or rather, pulled. When curled up asleep, as she often was with her tail dangling enticingly from the chair cushion, Tip, yielding to temptation, would take it in her mouth and pull it like a bell rope. The thud of Charlotte hitting the carpet and the sleepy 'Mrrr' as she climbed back up again plus loud, shuddering snores from Jess, were sounds I grew very used to during long winter evenings when awaiting Gordon's return from work.

Then it was March and both dogs came in season at the same time. As anyone knows, at that critical time an animal will be off like a shot in search of a mate, and two dogs on the rampage are a potential danger. Therefore, much to their disgust, Jess and Tip were clipped to their respective chains, unless I was working outside when I allowed one or the other, but never both together, to accompany me.

For some time a small brown village dog had haunted us.

He was firmly discouraged by our two who warned him in no uncertain terms that he was trespassing on their property. Suddenly, however, and much to his gratification their attitude changed completely. They actually welcomed him with squirms and wagging tails thinking he was not a bad looking fellow, actually, and it was nice of him to call. Couldn't *think* what they'd had against him before. So the day Tip and I were in the orchard tussling with yellow-elastic nettle roots and his sturdy little form appeared trotting importantly over the footbridge, I wasted no time but chased him off villagewards. Satisfied, I returned to the orchard — and found Tip gone.

I couldn't believe that she had left the farm. It had been no more than a couple of minutes since I had left her but though I called and whistled in every direction there was no response other than a wide-awake wuff from Jess.

At first, though perturbed, I was not unduly worried, feeling certain that she had made off to her favourite digging ground by the waterfall and thinking harsh thoughts I abandoned the nettles and gave chase.

The day was wild, windy and exceedingly noisy. My ears, straining to catch Tip's rabbiting voice, were startled by the crack of a shotgun and I stopped dead in my tracks. Gunshots are not uncommon in the country and this one might mean only the demise of some unsuspecting rabbit or bird, but the sound heightened my apprehension.

Because of the distorting influence of the wind I wasn't sure where the shot came from and it wasn't repeated but I thought it seemed to be in the direction of Ellers Farm above the forest. I changed course, running across the hayfield towards the forest fence. I tumbled over the barbed wire and climbed upwards over the line of our waterpipe, fighting my way through last year's arching bramble briars and reaching the top breathless and with thumping heart.

Nothing unusual was to be seen. Sheep at the far end of the field grazed peacefully. There was no dog among them, nor did I see any human though I waited and watched for some time. The shot, I decided with relief, was from somebody potting pigeons, and I turned back to descend through the forest.

Back in the valley the boys were returning from school.
'Tip's got away,' said Robert. 'Mr Arrowsmith says he has just seen her and another dog running through his big field!'

My heart plummeted again. Will's farm was far away from Stoney Flatt Foss. I brought the boys up to date with the news as we climbed the hill to Castle Farm. The dogs, needless to say, were no longer there but had been seen farther up the road by the gate to the Waterboard property. Pauline joined us and helped with the search. We called and whistled with the only result that the Castle Farm dogs eagerly joined us too.

'Let's go home,' said Antony. 'I bet she's there when we get back.'

I hoped she might be too, but she wasn't. Gordon was. Home early for once, and looking forward to a restful evening, he had just put one foot outside the car when he saw us hurrying up. He withdrew the foot as I incoherently poured out the story. I slid in beside him and for the rest of the evening and long after it was dark we drove up and down all the roads in the district. Frequently we stopped and got out into the starlight to whistle and listen. But nothing moved.

After a sleepless night, Gordon and I came downstairs early. Tip was not there. I rang the local policeman. Not to worry, he said. No trouble had been reported. He'd keep his eye open for them but they'd probably be back in an hour or so.

Only slightly cheered I was unable to settle to work and passed most of the morning wandering about wringing my hands in a frenzy of frustration. Then, about midday, PC Preston called to tell me that a sheep had been found worried up on the high moor in the next parish.

I must have looked as stricken as I felt because the policeman said kindly, 'Look now, wait and see. It might not be *your* dog.'

But I knew it was. It wasn't likely that other dogs were adrift on just that particular day. I felt sick with misery, worry and fatigue.

Later that afternoon the constable returned with both dogs in custody. They had killed two sheep and torn wool off a third. He had told the farmer that we had done everything possible to prevent this happening, and the farmer had agreed to settle for the price of one sheep from us and one from Ken Stubbs, the owner of the other dog.

Still trying to ease the way for me he went on. 'Look, he has dogs of his own that could do the same thing. He understands. It'll all be forgotten in a day or two. *But,*' he paused significantly, 'you know what this means?'

Sadly we did. That was the last afternoon in the lives of poor Tip and her friend. They paid dearly for their adventure.

20   A fowl tale

About this time an unusual assortment of birds chose — as that rather macabre expression has it — to die on us. Strictly speaking the owl died on the Arrowsmiths, but Robert and Antony were up at Castle Farm when the great bird fell to the ground at their feet. They all but went up into the air with shock themselves, said Robert. They thought it was some sort of an animal (a werewolf, said Antony) making a surprise attack. When they brought it home to show us, we saw what they meant.

Although we had an owl of our own, a superior bank manager type of bird called, inappropriately, Sam, who could be glimpsed sitting aloofly at the top of the yew tree by day, and heard holding board meetings on our chimney at night, we had never had the opportunity to examine one so closely before. Its legs encased in down as thick as fur looked more like rabbit's legs than a bird's. Why he should have dropped from the sky like that he gave no clue, but even bank managers, we are told, are mortal and we supposed that his time had come.

The next visitor from the sky dropped at *my* feet — this time a seagull who with bad error of judgment blundered into a tree and fell with what seemed to be a broken neck. I picked it up and its head lolled helplessly over my hand. Horrified, I tried to brace myself to put it out of its misery when to my overwhelming relief I saw the roadmen strolling over the footbridge. Thankfully, I raced across and handed over the job to Arnold.

For its last resting place the third corpse chose the duckhouse, of all places. About to close the door for the night, I noticed a mound of brown feathers lying unnaturally still in the nesting box.

That it was anything other than one of the Khaki Campbells never crossed my mind as I bent and picked it up, so when I saw what it was I was holding in my hands, I was, for a moment, stupefied. I seemed to see the metamorphosis actually taking place, the body rearranging its shape, the wide bill drastically altering, so that what I was holding was not a comfortable old duck but a streamlined wicked-beaked female sparrow-hawk. Quite dead.

Of *course* they hadn't put it there, said everyone indignantly when I, jumping to the wrong conclusion as usual, stormed around accusing them. Mother held the only clue. She had seen a large bird, a stranger to her, swoop low over the garden, bumble over the garden gate and fly clumsily down the yard.

In my experience dead sparrow-hawks, like dead postboys and donkeys, were things, as Sam Weller so astutely observed, that 'no man never see'.

It made a welcome change when the fourth *rara avis* opted to live, rather than die on us though this, need I say, posed further problems. Gordon first noticed this one as he crossed the bridge one evening on his way home from work. Delightedly he called me outside to see what he had found swimming in the beck. Some sort of duck, he explained happily, as I hurried towards the water.

Incident prone as we are, I mentally prepared myself for

something exotic like a red-necked grebe or black-browed albatross and I wasn't disappointed. What did surprise me was the creature's unprepossessing appearance, for contrasting indecently with its snow-white body, was an apoplectic scarlet face and bill. It was like nothing either of us had seen before.

Finding us equally unattractive it kept the full width of the beck between itself and us, swimming agitatedly back and forth below the farther bank and hissing at us in a far from friendly manner.

This was all very well but darkness was closing in and Gordon's evening meal was long overdue again. Yet we could hardly abandon the duck to fate and the night though, we didn't doubt, ingratitude be our only reward.

Why everybody had to choose us for foster parents, said Gordon as he stepped gingerly down the opposite bank and into the water, he didn't know. That was something else he had been saying for years. Back in Hull all the stray cats, dogs and budgerigars of the city used to turn up on our doorstep — I've been involved in many a canine conflict while walking dogs home on bits of string. Gordon swore that they turned them out of the Dogs' Home, told them Bellfield Avenue and slapped their bottoms to send them on their way. An opinion coloured perhaps, by the fact that I had so many times fed his dinner to these poor waifs.

In this instance the duck wasn't all that keen to be adopted by us. It didn't really fancy us at all and wasn't going to fall for being coaxed with bits of bread. When Gordon unfairly took it by surprise from the rear, however, it had no option but to swim across to where I waited hanging from a rhododendron on the orchard shore saying helpful things like, Mind you don't slip, Gordon. Be careful. Don't get wet, and the like.

Between us the duck was captured and locked into the hut with our lot who, because of the darkness, were unable to distinguish and discriminate against its colour.

Next morning, after attending to the stock and seeing the family off to its various destinations, I set about tracing the duck's owner. The postman started off the chain of telephone calls when he told me that Mrs Stewart had some fancy-looking ducks and why didn't I ring her? So I did. I described the bird's strange appearance. I wondered, I said, if it might have been a Muscovy? No, said Mrs Stewart, she had some of those and they weren't like that.

'A *red* face?' she said. She sounded puzzled. 'Has it been fighting and brought blood then?'

It was naturally red, I told her.

Well, that stumped her, she said. Couldn't think what it could be. But why didn't I ring Mr Hewson. He had all sorts of queer ducks up there ....

'A *red* face?' said Mr Hewson. 'What sort of red?'

'Bright red,' I answered. 'Scarlet red. I had wondered if it was a Muscovy but Mrs Stewart says not.'

No, he also had some o' them and their faces weren't red. Likely it had been rooting in t'river bank and got earth on its face.

Well, the soil is reddish here and there but not, I told him, tomato coloured. 'It's *naturally* red,' I said wearily, and rang off.

I phoned two more farmer neighbours who were united in their conviction that it wasn't a Muscovy and variously suggested that I phone the police and the nearest zoo.

Rather to my surprise the policeman said he had had a report of a missing pet duck and gave me the telephone number of a lady in a village a few miles away, but hers was nothing like ours.

That left the zoo. Luckily the number was engaged or goodness knows what I might have got involved in; the combination of us and a zoo doesn't bear thinking about. I intended to phone again later but before I had chance to do so I had a visitor, Charlie Rawdon, whom I had not contacted because Ellers Farm had no telephone.

He supposed I didn't happen to have seen owt of a duck, had I? he asked. I seized on him joyfully. I had, I had!

As he made his way over the wath, the duck safely contained in a sack, I had a sudden thought and shouted after him. 'What sort of a duck is it, anyway?'

He stopped in midstream and turned round slowly. 'It's

called a Muscovy', he said, pronouncing each syllable clearly for the benefit of my ignorance. 'A Mus-co-vy!' He continued over the wath.

'But ...' I began.

His voice wafted back from the other side of the beck. 'But it ain't a duck. He's a drake!'

21 Sheep may safely graze

When reading a book do you pause, as I do, to wonder what the author looks like? Idealising the creator of that tough, swash-buckling hero to be a Sean Connery in his own right, then seeing his picture in the press, all Adam's apple and no chin, and feeling let down over it? Well, I'll put you straight about me right away so that there will be no recriminations if we happen to bump into one another in the post office.

For a start my mouth isn't straight. Well, I knew it wasn't and thought that the dentist ought to have taken that into account when many years ago, he made me a small one-tooth denture. When I complained that it made me look like Dracula he came all over huffy and said that the denture wasn't at fault it was my mouth that was lopsided.

When I was being fitted for a maternity corset I was upbraided by the corsetiere for having an unusually long body. It had, she said, thrown all her measurements out.

The optician told me stiffly that the reason I couldn't focus through my first pair of reading glasses was that my eyes were set too close together. I gathered from his manner that he'd never seen anything like them outside the police courts. Personally, I wouldn't trust anyone who looks like me.

To add insult to injury my own family now accuse me of always standing with bent knees and round shoulders. The bowed shoulders tell their own story. My knees are bent to brace myself for the next shock that fate will dole out.

If you add to these imperfections my shuffling gait, you will have a very clear picture of me.

(In my defence I must point out that the shuffle is shared by all our family. It comes of perpetually wading through hens in the yard and cats in the kitchen.)

For my sagging knees and shoulders sheep must take the greatest share of the blame. For almost the whole of our first two years at Westwath my world revolved around them. They dictated when I should sleep, when I should eat, and when — the far, far greater fraction of my time — I should trudge up the hill to Castle Farm, their favourite trespassing ground, from whence we would return *en bloc* to the inconvenience of other road-users and with maximum embarrassment to me. I didn't have to go up there every day, of course. Sometimes Pauline would drive them down to me. Either way the traffic and my nerves suffered.

There was only one thing more aggravating than our sheep getting out and that was other people's sheep getting in. This last nuisance still persists long after our own flock has been sold and dispersed. The worst time for this is early spring when the fields are greening up, yet there is still very little to be had on the moor. At this time of the year we must be alert if we want the grass to grow long enough for hay.

That particular spring nearly led me to ovicide or whatever the murder of sheep is called. It began as usual with someone — Robert, this time — seeing a ewe in the top field, chasing it out and away up the moor. The following day the same thing happened; on the third the ewe brought reinforcements in the shape of another ewe and two hoggs (last year's lambs), all of them nibbling at the grass with the urgency of last minute shoppers on closing time.

Jess and I got them out that time. Afterwards we walked the field's boundaries, building up a bit of wall here, lifting a wire there and generally making the whole thing tight and sheep-proof. So tight and sheep-proof, in fact, that next day there were seven of them firmly dug in there.

Those seven were to needle us for weeks. Every day, with

Jess's cooperation, we turned them out and drove them over the moor to beyond the horizon, then we doggedly toured the defences again, carefully scrutinising every inch in the vain hope of discovering where they got in. We knew where they got out all right, but that proved nothing. Their exit point was a section of wall that had foot-holds in plenty on the field side of it but was close-set and beetling at the other.

The wall was as tall as I was, and heightened further by a run of barbed wire threaded through the twiggy branches of the hawthorn, rowan and birch trees that overhung it. The wire was fringed along its length with pulled out wool where the blighters had sailed over it. That weekend Gordon stretched another strand of barbed wire between posts planted outside the wall and made a double barrier. I gathered stone and heightened the wall yet another foot. We surveyed the result with satisfaction, confident that we had capped the so-and-sos this time. In this we were right in part. Only six sheep got in that night.

I spent hours patrolling those fields, and the month being Janus-faced April, sometimes the weather cooperated and sometimes it did not. As, for instance, the time a gale sprang up when I was ramming thorn branches between the wire and the wall, and I was punctured in so many places I looked like a nutmeg grater. Thatching a two hundred yard run of wall uses a lot of thorn bushes. I soon cleared the immediate vicinity and started on those in the fields below, where Donald the bullock, interfering as usual, actually got his nose nicked by my saw. I tied a rope around the branches and dragged them up the hill, where what little breath I had left was snatched out of my lungs by the wind, which having got it, didn't want it, and made me swallow it again. Jess's ears streamed out behind her and her long hair was flattened so close to her body that she looked like a whippet. She lay like a windswept sphinx on the spiky stalks of last year's bracken and kept diligent watch for sheep.

When April showed her good face and deigned to smile, conditions improved a little. Not much, but a little. One evening in particular I remember vividly.

Antony came home from school and reported that he had

turned the sheep out of the garage field, but they had doubled back and gone up the Scar. Shortly afterwards I went to check on them, found them in the Scar field and dogged them through the cattle grid. After tea we all took turns to chase them again. With binoculars I watched them file out of sight over the rim of a gully, after which I spent a pleasant quarter of an hour observing the countryside and reaffirming my opinion that it was a view to compare with the best in England.

On this still sunny April evening, moor, forests and fields were sharply defined in the clear warm light. Far away over the water-soughing ravine and the larch forest, hazily golden with breaking leaf buds, Will Arrowsmith was spreading manishment. Panning the binoculars across the extensive arcing boundary of the very ancient king's deer park that encircled Castle Farm I picked out Charlie Rawdon gathering in his cows for milking. Above me, black specks against the blue sky, larks ascended in hesitant vertical flight like lifts stopping at every floor, and the lately returned cuckoo called idiotically, eliciting an even more moronic response from me.

Knee deep in heather gruff voiced sheep replied to the baby cries of their lambs and were rewarded with hard little heads biffing their udders. Emotionally I sang aloud a few lines from 'Sheep May Safely Graze' then came right down to earth and the present time when I dropped my sights into the Westwath valley and saw my youngest child lying full length on the wath, swishing jersey-clad arms up to the elbows in the river.

And no sooner had I dealt with that — swopping wet clothes for pyjamas — when Robert dashed in saying that he had just seen my woolly friends swarming in again. Not over the wall from the moor, but up the steep face of the Scar.

'But I've just driven them half-way to Edinburgh,' I screamed. 'Besides, they can't get *up* there!'

But they had and were safely grazing like anything.

I ought to take a tent and camp up there I thought vexedly as I toiled up the hill again. This time we chased them three-quarters of the way to Edinburgh and dusk was thickening rapidly as Jess and I dragged ourselves homewards.

The royal-blue sky was sparsely perforated with marcasite points. Unseen, a pair of curlews bubbled and a whole army of owls hooted from every stand of trees. Of human presence little lingered, only a desultory chinking sound of unknown origin from the direction of Rowan Head and a few abstracted whistled phrases borne on the air from Castle Farm. Night was giving itself over to the wild creatures. And other animals, as I discovered when I glanced casually over the top field wall and counted seven sheep pottering about as if undisturbed for hours.

22 *'Lhude sing cuccu'*

I hadn't gone round the bend after all, I realised after a moment's reflection. Half an hour before, we had sent them charging over the horizon, and what must have happened was that the moment they were out of sight they had wheeled Scarwards and while Jess and I trudged homeward along the road, they had skipped along the face of the ravine, below and parallel to us, arriving in time to scramble up and over before we showed up. Don't tell me sheep are daft.

Apart from a break at lunchtime I spent the whole of the following day fencing along the top of the Scar. As you must know by now the Scar is a glacial ravine, deep, steep, sheer and rugged. The left hand side one of our pair of top fields totters on the Scar's brim, and to divide the field from space a stone wall tightrope walks along the edge. Over the wall the clifftop is less than a yard wide in at least two places and little more over the rest. From this fringe of terra — and far from — firma sprout several insecure-looking trees, most of them — not surprisingly — more bent-kneed than I am.

Visible here and there between their rickety legs was a

width of wire sheep netting and I remembered that one of the first jobs Gordon had done three years before was to renew the whole fence — along the top where I stood, down the bank where it plunged to the road, and the short section between the bank and the bridge. That short bit needed frequent renewal because it incorporated a stile which was regularly damaged by walkers.

At the first inspection — carried out while passing myself hand over hand monkeywise from one slender hazel trunk to another — I was convinced that nothing made of flesh and blood *could* climb up there, but halfway along I came to a fenceless gap between two jutting rocks. Looking down between them at the caved-out shaley cliff I was equally positive that nothing short of rising mist could get up it until — in my now well learned role of Hawkeye, the Indian scout — I spotted a couple of dents scored, I knew fatalistically, by animal hooves.

At the same time I saw the reason for this break in the defences. A dismayingly long way below, lying aslant in a bush was a sheet of rusty corrugated iron. Obviously it had once bridged the gap between the two rocks until some landslide had dislodged it. Fortunately for Gordon who otherwise would have been lumbered again, while I clung to my tree wildly casting around for a good reason for going home and forgetting about it, the Sickening Seven entered the stage again. They trooped on in single file from behind a rocky bluff, looking like the ladies of the chorus about to burst into song.

It was their insufferable aura of self-confidence that made me blow my top. Shouting fighting words like 'Hoya, hoya, hoya! Shoo! Scram! Clear off, you old faggots. Clear off. Clear *off!*' I pelted them with sticks, stones and everything I could lay my hands on.

Jess, recognising a funny turn when she saw one, hoisted herself to her feet and moved off a few paces to sit in a patch of bracken under the wall from where she could watch and criticise.

The sheep were leaving. Not running exactly, but they had changed direction slightly. A temporary victory for me but I recognised the stark fact that unless I replaced that sheet of iron the battle was as good as lost. I went home for a rope and a bundle of binder twine.

My first plan went like this. I would tie one end of the rope to a tree then slide down the cliff and tie the other end to the tin sheet. Then I'd climb back up the rope and haul it and the sheet up after me. But wait. What if I missed the hazel bush that held the sheet and went tobogganing on? I shouldn't enjoy the rough ride to the beck which, from where I crouched, was a glittering gash between tooth-like boulders. I modified the plan and tied the free end of the rope to me.

Secretly I was rather pleased about this because it meant a practical use for a bowline at last. We had learned to tie a bowline in the Sea Rangers, in case we ever had to be pulled up a cliff, and I was rather proud of mine. I could do one around my waist using only one hand and with my eyes closed. The other hand, we were told, would be holding on to a ledge and our eyes were closed so that we could do it in the dark. That the cliff would ever be other than hypothetical I couldn't foresee, and a cliff in the abstract, I now realised, was very different from one — as it were — in the flesh, but to my self-satisfaction I accomplished the descent without any trouble and glanced hopefully around for admiring onlookers. There were none. Jess was still there above me but her expression was discouraging to say the least. Her ears were flat in an attitude of no confidence and if she could have covered her eyes she would.

Working the baler band under and around the corrugated sheet was not easy because the iron was so eaten away by rust that the twine kept snagging, but I secured it eventually and tackled the ascent.

Now I was glad of no audience. My feet skidded on the loose shale and soil, the cliff jumped out and hit me and I slid down to the hazel bush again on my front. I saw a lot of that hazel bush during the next ten minutes, and all the time the cuckoo made maddening remarks which, under the circumstances, I took personally.

It was some time before I heaved myself onto the grass

beside Jess who had dropped her nose on her paws and was showing the whites of her eyes. She wasn't half relieved when I rolled over.

Thought I'd had it that time, she said, handing out accolades with her tongue and enthusiastically sniffing me all over to see where I'd been.

At the end of the day I had used just about every knot, bend and splice in my repertoire and had a tangle of netting up there, enough to fit out a fleet of trawlers. Thrusting out from it over the ravine were the last of the thorn bushes augmented by everything twiggy and spiky I could find. Short of melted lead and boiling oil there was nothing more I could do.

I slept well that night and next day caught up on a few things that had been neglected because of the sheep. Watering seedlings for instance, which because of the dry season were fast shrivelling away.

Also, owing to the lack of rain, the grass wasn't growing very well, and we were still feeding hay to the calves. So much so that all last season's good hay had been eaten and we were using up the dusty remains of the previous one. That haytime had been exceptionally wet and, country wide, people were handling dusty, mouldy fodder, prompting a spate of publicity about the disease called farmer's lung. I happened to clear my throat while Gordon was reading an article about it in the *Farmers' Weekly* and the next thing was he'd whipped me up a smog mask out of gauze, wadding and elastic. Wearing it I looked set to perform an appendectomy at least. It *was* a good idea though, I thought that lunchtime as, smothered in my armful of loose hay, I bounced with Bruno across the field.

On the way back I noticed a long ash stave leaning against the wall. On it somebody had nailed the flag I had found in the attic. We were looking out for good stout poles to raise another barbed wire above the top field wall and this, with the flag removed, would be admirable.

Thinking thus, I instinctively raised my eyes to those high fields across the road — and *saw there, peacefully grazing, seven blasted rotten sheep.*

I went berserk. Seizing the pole I panted up the hill, across the road and over the Scar field gate. The sheep fled at the sight of me, swarming over the far back wall amid a shower of stones, and were gone before I had taken a dozen steps into the field. I ran up to the wall and pelted the stones after them, yelling all the abuse I could think of. I felt exhausted after that.

I turned and started back down the field. There were two cars, barely moving, on the hill. Their occupants were staring in a way I knew only too well. This time I couldn't blame them, for what they had witnessed — and the realisation hit me like a sledgehammer — was a crazy woman screaming across an empty field, wearing a smog mask and waving a Union Jack.

Lhude sing cuccu.

23 Haec olim meminisse juvabit

It really was too much, I wailed to Gordon that night. Those devils of sheep were driving me *mad*. What on earth must people *think*? I couldn't stand much more, I told him.

So on the following afternoon, a Saturday, Gordon and I drove over to see Bill Dawson, the owner of the sheep. Why we hadn't done this before I cannot now remember. I had sent messages both written and verbal, ranging from the light casual through crisp tartness to downright entreaty without, I had thought, arousing any response.

However, it appeared that in this I was wrong. Bill had been down on several occasions and driven the sheep out but with no more lasting success than we'd had. Willingly he and John, his neighbour's son, returned with us to Westwath for the great round-up. We planned to pen the sheep in the small enclosure of our now disused sheep dip, nab the two prime movers of the mob and Bill would take them away in his van.

It was tough from the start. Once over the wall the gang, briefed by the ring leaders, scattered in all directions while we, dogs and humans, ran, leaped gullies, grabbed wool, jumped rocks, splashed in streams, barked knuckles and swore. We had villains in our old flock but none so steeped in crime as these. To add to the chaos a mist was gathering in.

At this point I bowed out. Not intentionally, I hasten to explain, but I returned home with Roger who had kindly toddled up with offers of help. By the time I came back the action had changed its location and I got lost in the fog looking for it.

Gordon told me the end of the affair later.

The sheep, it transpired, would go nowhere near the dipping pen but, having fortuitously rounded them up in a bunch on the roadway, Bill changed his mind about using the van and marched them all off along the mile long road to the village instead.

It wasn't easy, said Gordon, because the sheep, escapists to a woman, continually darted off into the fog, so everybody breathed a sigh of relief when they reached Bill's barn and shot the blighters inside.

And then, said Gordon, I'd never believe it but the next second, just as he was beginning to relax, the blasted animals barged straight through a door at the farther end and the two leaders jumped a wall as tall as himself and scarpered up the road again. Gordon closed his eyes and shuddered at the awful memory.

Yes, he replied wearily in answer to my desperate query. They *had* caught them again and locked them in the barn. *And* tethered them for good measure. I hoped it was to a ball and chain and their feet set in concrete.

Now the reason I was so late returning to the others and consequently missing the capture, was this. When I returned home with Roger reluctantly in tow, I found we were being attacked in the rear by five of Mr Stewart's heifers who had forded the beck and were making themselves very much at home in our vegetable garden. It was one of those regularly recurring days when I wonder why I am an animal lover. That afternoon Robert was at Castle Farm, Antony was recovering from his latest accident and Jess, of course, was helping Gordon with the sheep. So it fell to me to do the running, barking and wading necessary to return the trespassers to their own side of the water. It was with lessened enthusiasm I swished through the fog-entangled heather in the direction in which I thought the sheep hunt had gone. It hadn't. Well, I never dreamed they had gone *home*. So I kept on following my nose and imagined voices until I was way off course and all alone wrapped in a clammy white blanket of mist, feeling extremely fed up and frustrated.

Not worried though because, although I couldn't see a blooming thing, children's shouts and laughter carrying from Castle Farm a mile or so away in one direction, and the faint periodic chiming of the church clock in another gave a near enough indication of my position. Which was vastly more comfortable than that in which I found myself many years ago when I really *was* lost on these Yorkshire moors.

There were two of us, my friend Mary, and myself. We were out for a long weekend's Youth Hostelling holiday and the whole thing happened because I couldn't find my compass. This was strange because I always carried it about with me as it made me feel nautical.

The first night we spent at Lastingham, the second at Wheeldale, and between these places part of the route follows the Roman road, so that day a compass was superfluous anyway. We intended to spend the third night at Filey and had planned a pleasant walk across the moor to a point some miles north of Scarborough where we would join the main road and stroll into the town for afternoon tea before catching a bus to our destination.

We studied our one inch to the mile Ordnance Survey map and traced the staccato line which darted confidently eastwards across the moor to join up, eventually, with other stuttering lines — a veritable Piccadilly Circus. One of these paths was even distinguished by a name — Robin Hood's Bay Road. Perfectly straightforward according to the map.

The Dr Who setting of the Early Warning Station had not

yet been constructed but for some years Flyingdales moor had been used for army training. This was October, however, manoeuvres were over for the season and there were no red warning flags flying.

We stopped for elevenses in the lee of Lilla Howe, the mound (which would have been surmounted by a stone cross if it had not, for safety's sake, been temporarily removed out of the military firing area) where was buried Lilla, a minister of King Edwin, who in saving his King's life had lost his own. Here according to the map was where the crossroads ought to be.

The footpath had deteriorated badly, thanks to the many tank tracks that crossed and recrossed it. Gamely it had struggled on until, in sight of Lilla Howe, it had lost the will to survive and gone completely to pieces. The same fate had overtaken the converging paths. Cross-rutted and oozing, Robin Hood's Bay Road was a morass. The place was a devastated area. In the hope of picking up the trail — *any* trail — we cast about in every direction including, I don't doubt, the one by which we had come. Because by then, we didn't know which that was either. Science was no help: there was no sun to get a fix by and a licked finger held up into the wind merely froze.

On every side, stretching away as far as the eye could see was a desolate landscape of dark undulating heather, wave after wave of it.

An uncertain fleeting shaft of sunshine encouraged us to break the impasse and set out in what we *hoped* was an easterly direction. Mostly it rained on us but sometimes it didn't. At those times we could see far over to the distant hills where it did. Then the hills would vanish again as the rain swept towards us and enveloped us. Mile after mile and hour after hour we trudged on, more than once confidently making for what we thought was a distant glimpse of the sea only to find that it was yet another mist-blurred range of hills.

Interspersed between tufts of charcoal heather, smooth emerald green mats of moss treacherously enticed us and sucked at our legs as we sank knee-deep in the bog which lay beneath. With boots oozing water, trouser-legs clinging clammily and noses perpetually running we were cold, tired and hungry.

Then: 'I can see a notice board,' said Mary in a mild conversational tone.

I blinked, for a moment convinced that the ordeal had proved too much for her. But, as I looked nervously in her direction, I saw the notice board, too.

'Saved!' I yelled and beat Mary to it by a short head. I began to read it aloud, joy ebbing out as the words sank in. 'Explosives. It is Dangerous to Enter Here.'

'Oh,' said Mary shortly — she was never demonstrative.

At that moment I felt in my pocket for my handkerchief for the hundredth time that day and pulled out — the compass. To this day I can't explain it.

Mary didn't attack me — not even verbally — but she snatched the compass from my hand and set off madly in an easterly direction with me treading her boots down at the back. Straight on we went, through swamps, reeds, waist high heather and — for all we knew — an arsenal of unexploded bombs, until a line on the far horizon was positively identified as the sea. We reached the road eventually and rolling towards us, right on cue, was a beautiful red bus. Oh poop, poop!

At Scarborough we limped into the bus station ladies room. A middle aged flowered and feathered lady, unmistakably a recent wedding guest, pirouetted on her toes with arms outstretched.

'Hasn't it,' she cried ecstatically, 'been a *wonderful* day.'

24 Tails you win

Disencumbered of sheep we were free to turn our attention to matters that had been pressing us for some time. Winter rains and melting snow had been too much for the little stream which, tumbling out of the forest by way of a verdant waterfall, flows between the back and holme fields. Dammed by a washed-out tree stump, the waters had spread to flood the far end of the fields, the part that even in the driest of summers, is inclined to be boggy. The receding water had left a scene like a map of the Irrawaddy Delta. Between the fan of twisting channels, mudflats were scored and ridged by smaller runnels and resembled the bony fins of a skate. It smelled like a skate too. One that had been misplaced for a very long time. Gordon couldn't tackle it before the weekend but I made a start on Thursday morning.

I began by digging a narrow shallow ditch over the stream's original course and finding, as always, that it was a harder job than I had envisaged. To start with the spade wouldn't go in because of the long grass and tough marsh marigold stalks embedded in the mud infill. When I did manage to scoop up a spadeful the stuff was so glutinous that it wouldn't come off again without a struggle. To do the job at all I had to stand astride the so-called stream and dig down between my feet, heaving the awful smelling stuff out and dumping it on one bank.

I didn't lose my boots *all* the time. It just seemed like it. Memory evokes numerous pictures of me standing slimily barefoot as I wrested wellies from the stream's miry clutches.

Jess lay on the nearest firm ground and watched hopefully. Each time I did something fairly interesting like losing a boot or overbalancing into a croquet hoop attitude, elbow-deep in water, she wagged her tail politely but was obviously saving her applause for the better entertainment of which, she knew, I was capable.

The day was warm for late April and I took off my jersey, draping it over a handy blackcurrant bush, a relic of the original orchard. This pleased the midges no end and they made enthusiastic excursions over hitherto uncharted territory up the short sleeves of my blouse and down the back of my neck. Forgetting the state of my hands I slapped at the midges. This didn't improve my appearance at all. But I laboured on (in those days I used to drive myself to gargantuan efforts. Now I feel tired just remembering, and leave the strong man stuff to grown-up sons) until Mrs Dale opened her Diary at four o'clock.

That quarter of an hour with Mrs Dale was always sacrosanct. Feet up, a cup of tea, my worries swopped for hers and I was a different woman. How I miss her. Routine has never been the same since the programme was taken off the air.

I drank three cups of tea that Thursday afternoon to partially replace the gallons of liquid I had shed in perspiration, but I should have enjoyed it better dissociated from the gaseous smell which enveloped me. In the confines of the house I was very pungent indeed and Charlotte very pointedly walked off to revive herself on the doorstep. I dumped trousers, blouse and jersey outside the back door and went upstairs for a bath.

The bath was wonderful. I lay for ages soaking away the aches and pains wondering, as always, at the extraordinary variety of material that floated off me. On days such as that one the bath reminded me of Hull's old Princes Dock before it was closed to shipping. The dock used to be rimmed with driftwood and rubbish: the bath was the same with scaled down flotsam — leaves, straw, feathers and a wide selection of insects. A beachcomber's paradise.

It was fortunate that I enjoyed the bath when I did because had I decided to take it later in the evening I should have been very unlucky.

At ten o'clock, hot water bottle filling time, I found that the hot water tank was empty. The light from a waning torch revealed that there was nothing in the cistern in the attic either, and probably hadn't been since way back when I had my bath. And there was I with the Rayburn going great guns against the frosty night and the back boiler about to burst at any minute.

I know now that I could have drawn water from the cold tap in the bathroom but at that time our plumbing was as mysterious to me as the workings of an atomic plant and I daren't turn on a tap in case something frightful happened.

There was nothing else for it but to take a bucket to the independent tap down the yard.

Freezing it was, out there, and as black as pitch, the antithesis of the warm sunny afternoon gone by. The torch was practically useless — our battery consumption average being on a par with our intake of bandages — and the only sizeable bucket that came to hand had a weeping leak at the seam. Its diminished contents made a small puddle on the floor of the attic tank.

I was skating back up the yard on the second trip, mentally calculating the number of gallons it was possible to carry over fifty slippery yards, through five doors and up two flights of stairs before one's arm dropped off when, joy of joys, Gordon's headlights swept around and stopped by the garage. Five minutes after sizing up the situation he had water flooding normally into the tank.

Just as normally, when you consider the sort of things that happen to us, a few weeks later water was flooding out of it. That I just happened to be up there when it began was a slip up on the part of Fate who usually contrived to make things more difficult than that. I was scrubbing a hundred years-worth of whitewash off the attic beams when I first noticed the wet patch on the floorboards alongside the big square tank. My first thought was that I had been over enthusiastic with the use of the scrubbing brush but when the patch grew before my eyes although scrubbing was suspended, I knew it was going to be another of those days.

Sure enough, water was trickling down the side of the tank from what looked like a spot of rust. Tentatively I touched it with my finger. The rust dropped out under my finger (as you knew it would) and I was faced with an arching jet which speedily and considerably added to the expanding outline of the pool on the floor. I shouted through the attic window for Gordon to do what he had come to accept as the normal way of life — break off in the middle of one urgent job to attend to another.

The result of that little episode was a new tank, a large hole cut out of the floorboards to admit it, and the best part of a day's labour for Gordon to help fix it as the plumber had palpitations at the mere thought of doing it all by himself.

There was also a soggy carpet in the bedroom below. It was Robert and Antony's room. And, all credit due to Charlotte, it was Storky's, Butterscotch's and Blue Boy's bedroom too.

Charlotte, after weeks of the most brazen husband hunting, had at last landed one, although, I thought, as I watched the ginger tom streaking over the footbridge with Charlotte in hot pursuit, a more reluctant spouse would be hard to imagine. Drawn obviously by Charlotte's incredible voice he had fallen into the trap with the result that on the afternoon of Sunday, May twenty-fourth, nineteen hundred and seventy, Charlotte was brought to bed of two ginger daughters and one blue-grey son.

The kittens were born in a box which we had prepared in the back hall. Charlotte would like it there, we thought: private and undisturbed yet close enough for us to replenish her food dishes easily.

This sort of thing being infectious, two days later Rhoda also chose to introduce her new calf who let me know how things stood from the off when, within minutes of getting onto his feet for the first time, he lowered his head very bull-fashion and sized up to me in what he expected was a menacing manner. It might have been too, if his legs hadn't treacherously crossed, letting him down ignominiously into the buttercups. I knew we had a right one here when less than a couple of hours later he broke out of his pen and was found blissfully suckling his mother in the cowhouse.

That was the day that Charlotte decided to move house. When she suddenly ran past me in the kitchen I merely registered that she was in a bit of a hurry and went on washing up. It was mother peeping into the back hall who noticed that one of the ginger kittens was missing. She lifted the woolly jersey which lined the box then searched around the hall but the kitten had vanished sure enough.

'Hidden it,' said mother admiringly. 'Crafty Clara.'

At that moment Charlotte strolled nonchalantly back. She walked into the hall and peered critically into the box of sleeping infants. She was horrified at what she saw.

Somebody had touched them. They were *filthy*. Amid a chorus of protesting pipings she climbed into the box and stropped them with a vigour that would have been better directed to rolling plasticine. Mother and I, feigning disinterest, returned to the kitchen and ostentatiously dried and put away the dishes.

Next minute Charlotte scurried determinedly past us with the grey kitten clenched in her mouth. We watched her hurry through the dining room and heard her patter up the stairs. I was just in time to see her disappearing into the boys' bedroom where, as I peered stealthily around the door jamb, she was found backing out from under the eiderdown with a brisk air of knowing a job well done.

And what did she think she was doing, I enquired as Charlotte jumped hastily to the floor. Her answer to that was to sit firmly down on her spine, stick out a back leg and wash it, conspicuously ignoring the bed. When I picked her up and peeled back the eiderdown revealing the cosy nest with its sleeping contents Charlotte craned her neck in astonishment. Just fancy that! Who would have thought it!

With my spare hand I gathered up the kittens, brought all three downstairs and dumped them into their lawful bed with dire warnings what would happen if Charlotte did it again. This worried her so much that we arrived at the kitchen in a dead heat. It was the ginger kitten again, I saw, when its loving mother accidently dropped it on the concrete floor. We both made a grab for it. Charlotte won and raced through the dining room to the now closed stair door where I captured them both.

How Storky grew up to be the intelligent creature she is — or ever grew up at all — is a miracle. She was dragged out of the box half a dozen times and once, because someone accidentally left the doors open, she was hauled all the way back to the bedroom again hitting every stair on the way and, because her mother had omitted to put her down before turning to argue with me, was dropped from bed height for good measure.

We compromised in the end — Charlotte insisting on the bedroom or nothing and us agreeing to it.

But not *in* the bed itself, I insisted, placing the kittens, box and all on top of the spare bed.

Not that bed, said Charlotte equally adamant. *That* one. In the end I stripped off the boys' bed and made up the spare one for them, and Charlotte and her family settled in on top of the other.

At last, sighed Charlotte, turning the kittens on their backs and changing their nappies. Honestly, some people were so *thick*.

Storky's full name and style is Storky Floorcloth MP,CC, TC. Storky, because she and her sister were so alike that Gordon named them Stork and Butter; Floorcloth, because of the way Charlotte wiped her over the carpet. MP stood for Mother's Pet which she so clearly *was*, a favour she could easily have foregone, entailing as it did, such a touch and go existence. CC was for Cow Cat because she wouldn't dream of letting Jess bring home the cows without her support and assistance, and TC was Tractor Cat. As the first peace shattering roar of the old tractor's engine reverberated through the blameless countryside Storky would leave whatever business she had in hand and rally to the call. No matter what was going on she had to be in on it. She still carries a legacy of her mother's passion for portage in the conspicuous twirl of fur on the back of her neck. This was useful in the early days when it helped to distinguish her from her sister, Butter.

Butter — or Butterscotch — is deaf, a handicap we knew nothing of for some time. As a small kitten she was only slightly less of a dare-devil than her brother and sister who, when they weren't trying to kick each other's ears off, were flying around the house like jet propelled monkeys playing first one to touch the floor is out. Their entertainment value was beyond price — and so was the damage to the chair covers. No house should be without at least three kittens, we said, holding our sides as the trio, springing from three separate ambushes, collided a couple of feet in the air with the sound and impact of thistledown.

I didn't say that the time they all in sequence, during a rip-roaring circuit of the kitchen, touched down on my back as I crouched to lift a tray of buns from the oven. It didn't improve matters either, when Robert, helping to pick the broken cakes out of the hearth, reassured a visiting acquaintance that it would be all right. They wouldn't waste because mum would make them into chocolate truffles. He explained to the startled woman that I always did that when I dropped things. This was true as far as it went. I'd had a few spillages lately because, without realising it, I was becoming long-sighted and often misjudged the position of the chromium towel rail on the Rayburn's front, catching it with the baking trays. Sometimes a salvaged cake did appear in a new guise as chocolate truffles but the way Robert told it anyone would think I scooped up the lot, cinders and all, with a coating of ashes for chocolate vermicelli.

Considering that the kittens were no more than four inches tall and could walk under the sideboard with hardly a dip of their spiky little tails, it was surprising how much they made their presence felt. Charlotte was no help to us. Their egos would never suffer because of her. Only the best was good enough for her children and she let us know it. The bedroom had suddenly become unsuitable when the kittens were about a month old.

It was a disgrace, Charlotte informed us indignantly. All that overcrowding and no mod cons. Forthwith she hauled the lot of them downstairs again and installed them on the pouffe by the Rayburn.

From then on it became the regular thing for Charlotte to appear on the outside windowsill uttering muffled cries for admittance. Muffled because she was talking through a mouthful of mouse and grass — meat and vegetables, we called it — which she had brought to supplement the kittens' milk diet. The kittens being only marginally larger than the mice at that time, they were not really interested, and the mice lay disregarded on the kitchen floor.

'And what,' I demanded of Charlotte, 'am I supposed to do with these?'

Charlotte sniffed them disinterestedly. Chocolate truffles? she suggested brightly.

25 Heads we lose

That year saw a significant improvement in our comfort for, by dint of much pinching and scraping, assisted by the newly extended home improvement grant which promised to pay fifty per cent of the cost, we were able to go ahead with the no longer postponable repairs to the house.

Running water in every room is not an advantage when the walls are the source of it. Likewise, a roof partially open to the sky might be an advantage in, say, Tunisia but it will never be successful around here. The mere thought of another winter like the last three, when a few clothes drying in front of the fire or a Christmas pudding steaming on the stove overburdened an atmosphere so moisture-filled that it made that of the Amazon basin seem arid by comparison, caused us to come out in gooseflesh all over.

The joy with which we looked forward to the undertaking was not unalloyed. It meant, and our hearts dropped like stones at the thought, Having the Men In, and we had just had a pennyworth of that.

At long last the outer porch had been rebuilt after the snow damage — and we had hated every minute of it. The firm we had chosen to do the work had a very good reputation but unfortunately its best men had retired or gone off sick, and what we got was a couple of youngsters with whom we were totally incompatible. They idled away each day and were moved to frenzied activity only when their employer made his daily inspection. The erection of an eight foot length of guttering and a similar length of fallpipe occupied the two of them for an entire day — approximately an hour per foot. No, no, I must be fair — *half* an hour per foot. The rest of the time was tea break.

For all we knew we could have been out of the frying pan and into the fire when we asked a couple of other builders to estimate for the major repairs but finally we settled for Johnsons. We composed ourselves to wait until September, the month tentatively suggested by Mr Johnson for a starting date.

Not that everything could wait until then though. Gordon still had to do emergency repairs now and then to see us through. Like, for instance, the time I came downstairs one morning and found a great hole gnawed through the rotten front door jamb, and chewed up wood and leaves heaped up nest-like on the doormat. Whether it was a new rat coming in or our old one reconnoitring for fresh bedding we never knew. That we had at least one rat of our own we had known from the off, when a paper sackful of potatoes left trustingly on the pantry floor was found spilling its contents out through a ragged hole; each potato individually stamped with a sample bite. We knew he had found one to his liking when the bookcase fell through the sitting room floor and we found the potato behind the skirting board miles from its source in the paper bag. It was a big potato too. Heaven knew, said Gordon, the size of the rat.

Faced with a bookcase shaped hole in the floorboards Gordon was feeling aggrieved. The more so when he found that the floor joists, resting on the bare earth, had rotted away so completely at the ends that they stopped short a foot from the walls, all around the perimeter. We spent the rest of the day digging out and barrowing away the earth. This happened soon after we moved into Westwath, long before we could consider the professional installation of a damp course, so Gordon patched up the joists and laid new floorboards during the whole of one Sunday. Since then there had been a whole succession of temporary repairs including a roof patching job to carry us through the second winter.

Now, however, looking forward to these matters being taken care of more permanently by professionals, Gordon turned his attention to special details like the front door. The front door was a solid, four panelled affair with good brass furniture — a very nice door in fact — but one of the lower panels was badly cracked.

Now my husband is one of those commendable but aggravating people — a perfectionist. Which means that I have to wait ten times as long as women with less particular husbands for projects to be completed. Either he doesn't start on them at all (if a job's worth doing it's worth doing properly, and all that piping wants setting back *into* the wall, not disguising with paint) or else he does start and — as far as I can see — finish, then just as I am about to set things out on his new shelves/tables/cupboards I find they are all in pieces again. He was only offering them up, he explains.

So when he unhinged the front door and took it apart in the workshop I had an idea what we were in for. Even more so when he went to the trouble of making a frame and tacking a plastic sheet over it to fit in the aperture. At first this was satisfactory, except that the whole family couldn't go out together leaving the house unattended with nothing other than a sheet of plastic between a marauder and the egg money. But after being fretted by wind and rain for a week or so the sheet got decidedly raggy around the edges — a circumstance that Charlotte was quick to exploit.

It so happened that this was summer and the boys had moved up into the better end of the attic again, and the first we knew about Charlotte's enterprise was a series of bumps on our bedroom ceiling which seemed to go on all night. This — we learnt next morning having been too tired to investigate during the small hours — was the boys pushing Charlotte, Storky, Butterscotch and Blue Boy off their bed where Charlotte, having gained an entry for them all through a loose corner of the plastic door, intended they should sleep. As fast as they had pushed them off, complained Robert, they'd climbed on again. It wouldn't have been so bad, he said, if they hadn't made such a row purring.

The builders were due to start in September, but long before then the house got its new roof. The exercise involved the eviction of a number of squatter families. He'd never seen so many birds' nests in a roof, said the elder of the two workmen — thought at first it had been thatched underneath. He was tossing down nests of such obvious antiquity that I feared they might have had a preservation order on them. Luckily there were no unfledged birds in residence but there *was* a nest of baby bats. Where on earth, I thought helplessly, could I put them for safety? I investigated all the outbuildings with the cradle of babies cupped in my hands thinking that nothing could look more vulnerable — unless it was a nest of field mice rudely uncovered at haytime.

I settled in the end for a ramshackle hut near the vegetable garden, placing the nest on top of the frame under the broken overhanging roof where it was safe from Charlotte and the elements but easily accessible to the parents.

We spent the evenings of those three days on salvage work, sorting whole pantiles from broken ones for future use on the outbuildings. The old limewashed laths were gathered up and stacked for firewood except for some of the longer stouter ones which were spirited away by Robert for an unspecified purpose.

Very industrious we all were. Mother and Roger bagging up laths, Gordon and I chucking pieces of tile into the metal wheelbarrow which Gordon tipped down the yard. And Robert doing mysterious things with saw and hammer and — even more intriguing — a flat iron. The iron was one of a pair we had found in the attic. What Robert wanted it for we couldn't imagine, but all was revealed a few days later when we were all summoned to a grand launching ceremony. There, in the deep side of the beck, gently nudging the wath, floated an elegant canoe. With a frame of strong roofing laths and a skin of plastic fertiliser bags welded together with the hot flat iron it looked perfect.

But it wasn't quite, as Gordon abruptly found out when, with impressive parental responsibility, he insisted on first testing it out for seaworthiness.

Everyone stood around and watched with admiration as he stepped off the wath and lowered himself cautiously into the tiny cockpit. And everyone except Robert laughed like hyenas when, without so much as granting him time to nail his colours to the mast, the canoe took a sudden turn for the worse.

That little setback was easily remedied by the addition of stabilisers — two oil drums affixed one on either end of another length of lath and fastened athwartship across the gunnels like outriggers. The second launching went without mishap and started what came to be known as 'canoe summer' with everyone arguing for turns in *Swallow* until Robert, assisted by an enthusiastic Pauline, built a second canoe, *Amazon*, to ease the strain.

Eager though we were for the approach of autumn and the builders, the summer sped by leaping, as it were, from the summit of one crisis to the crest of the next; one of them the ever recurring natural hazard of the water supply which was becoming as much a summer institution as Henley Regatta. This year after we had emptied and scrubbed out the tank above the forest the kitchen tap reluctantly dispensed something that looked like cold cocoa.

As Gordon, making good use of a precious weekend, was fully occupied in constructing new calf pens, this new development left him — as he said himself — definitely unchuffed, which was nothing to what it left me. With two milking pails, six calf feeding buckets, one bottle and teat and a milk sile to wash and scald apart from all the usual domestic needs, I was very annoyed. A state of mind not improved by memories which flooded over me like a tidal wave. Memories of just such another situation three years before, when for a mosquito-ridden fortnight we crawled about in the sweaty undergrowth of the forest clearing silt out of the alkathene pipe.

That wouldn't be necessary this time, said Gordon, cheering me no end for all of two seconds. What we would do this time, he said, thereby squashing cheerfulness into the ground and stamping on it, would be to clear out the *rest* of the pipe where it crossed the field. The hundred yards or so that hadn't been done last time. So if I would like (would like, ha!) to find where it lay and uncover it in a few places while he carried on with the calf pens ....

True, the exercise turned out to be not nearly so exhausting as that earlier one but all these little upsets tell on one as one gets older, and I think I could have been excused when, later in the day, I got the wind up and alerted panic stations again.

The calves' watertap, said Gordon scathingly when he had heard my agitated report, was running hot *not* because he had accidentally joined it up to the boiler as I seemed to be inferring, but because the pipe had been lying in the sun all day.

I was jolly hurt by his manner, I can tell you.

26   The builders are coming

I was still a little unstable the next day which I began by brewing the tea with boiling milk, and Gordon deemed it prudent to establish the day's programme with me before he left for work.

I wouldn't forget, would I, he said anxiously, to order transport for the beasts to market. And to phone the A.I. for Rosie. And if there was time after whitewashing the cowhouse could I carry on digging the stream ...?

I said yes to everything although I had no intention of digging the stream with a muscle in my groin still adrift from my last stint. I hadn't told anyone about the muscle but went about with a brave smile and cheerful acceptance as is my wont.

The usual carrier couldn't manage to take our cattle that weekend. Nor could another firm I telephoned, so casting further afield, I rang Mr Hewson for recommendations.

The Hewsons, you will remember, lived at Rowan Head, the farmhouse sitting way above us right on the skyline on the rounded shoulder of a hill. For months at a time a solitary light powered by their generator shone like a leading light from the heights and was the only outside light we ever saw, a companionable sight on a dark, rainy winter's night. Any time, we could raise our eyes and see their cattle grazing, and sometimes their tractor, reduced by distance to the size of an ant, crawling up the steep hillside, but we seldom met the Hewsons themselves so we had a lot to talk about when I rang him with my inquiry.

I surprised him with the story of the waterpipe.

He electrified me with the news that the moor was on fire just behind our house.

It was all right. There was no need to worry, he said soothingly. It was all of half a mile away up by Killin Crag. He'd seen it start an hour ago and rung fire brigade. He reckoned it was them campers up be sheep beeld leaving bottles about. Some folks had no sense. All this sun and the moor tinder dry, it was just asking for it.

We talked a while longer although I was itching to be off to see the fire. From his high vantage point on the other side of the valley Mr Hewson was giving me a running commentary and I supposed that if the flames were lapping our doorstep he would tell me. All the same, I couldn't help thinking that half a mile wasn't much and I ought to be filling buckets or something. At least the beck was between it and us.

Any road, concluded Mr Hewson, he always had Huggetts to transport his cattle. He was a reliable feller and sure to fix us up. Glad to help, and anytime, *anytime* he could do anything for us I only had to give him a ring ....

I bet he didn't expect me to do it that very afternoon though.

I had been up in the forest. Because of the pain in my groin it had been an uncomfortable climb but I wanted to watch the progress of the fire from the grandstand height. It was the first proper moor fire I had seen, and with flames shooting to more than twice the height of the slight black figures of the beaters, I was greatly overawed.

Along the road that leads to the head of the valley, fire tenders were parked and a tractor towing what I presumed to be a tank of water struck across the heather and vanished in the smoke.

It was drifting northwards, away from us, so it seemed safe

to whitewash the cowhouse. It would have been a pity to waste the effort if it was going to be burned down in an hour or two.

Considering the reputed uneventfulness of country living we seemed to spend a disproportionate amount of time hoping we should survive another day. I hoped that even harder when I emerged from the forest straight into another rodeo. Half a dozen stirks had broken out of their field and were galumphing about in the next one — which only two days earlier Gordon had sprayed with weedkiller. The sort that has to be kept away from animals.

I leaped to the attack and my strained muscles ran knives up my side. Jess, steadfast to her principles and union rules, made off along the hedgerow — Didn't want *her* poisoning as well as the stirks, did I and her woolly black rump disappearing down the steps to the garden was the last I saw of her for some time.

That was all very well but if she wouldn't chase them out and I couldn't — and every step I took told me that — what was to be done? I daren't risk leaving them until the boys returned from school — that wouldn't be for hours. Neither could I run up to Castle Farm. Even as I considered it Agnes paused in mid buck and tore at a tempting mouthful of dandelion. I phoned Mr Hewson.

They soon had everything under control — Mr and Mrs Hewson, their dog and — Jess. Jess had the grace to throw me a jolly sheepish look as she tore past on the heels of the departing herd.

I knew what it was, of course. She was putting on a show for the benefit of the other dog. But she didn't half make me look a fool because I'd just finished explaining to the Hewsons how, although she was a wizard with sheep, cattlewise she wouldn't go near anything younger than a cow.

Back in their own field but bearing no malice, Agnes, Bruno, Donald and Co. raced back down its length parallel with the dogs who were returning equally friskily down the other. What the Hewsons were thinking of me was not apparent but I do know what I was thinking about Jess. She knew it too, and the closer she got the more embarrassed she became. By the time she had reached us her tail was between her legs with only the upturned end optimistically sweeping the ground. Her ingratiating manner as she wriggled around my feet outclassed Uriah Heep on all points. Even he didn't lie on his back hoping to have his chest scratched.

And so the summer passed and September came at last, a hot month all blue and gold. The day before the builders were due Gordon completed excavating the stream. Straight-edged and neat it firmly conducted the drainage water to the underground conduit which discharged into the beck. Pauline and Robert furthered the tidying up programme by pulling out old fence posts and dead wood which they then stacked on the sledge and led away — both by now being proficient tractor drivers — to the winter woodpile. I followed in their wake digging out rusty barbed wire which, disintegrating in the ground and mixing with the vegetation, can be swallowed by cattle, with painful and fatal results.

Afterwards I climbed up into the forest and took photographs.

The undergrowth was long and tangled with bramble briars, the fruit large, black and sweet. Cobwebs full of willowherb seed sagged like trawl nets with a bumper catch. Thickets of the weed stood taller than I, each spearhead softened with flannel-like peeled-back seed pods, and the air about was thick with expelled parachutes. It was to be a good seed year all round.

Down below, the trees in our orchard were drooping with fruit. A small boy, newly come to stay in the bungalow, was admonished by his father when he jumped, arms outstretched, to touch the temptingly dangling plums, 'Stop it, you've not come here to play. You've come on *holiday*.'

But this weekend had seen the last of the holiday visitors, and Gordon and I moved into the bungalow. And so did most of our furniture. For days now we had been playing Chinese chequers with beds, tables, chests and chairs in an attempt to clear a way for the builders. Only two rooms in the whole house were to be spared drastic renovation. For in order to qualify for the improvement grant, not only were the imperative roof renewal and damp course installation to be carried out but there were to be many more alterations and repairs necessary to bring the house up to the required standard.

Upstairs two bedrooms were to have their windows enlarged and the open raftered ceilings underdrawn. The third bedroom with the pine ceiling was to be untouched so in there went all the beds, wardrobes and chest of drawers. Slotted in there amongst them slept mother and all three boys.

Downstairs, the kitchen alone was exempt. As to the rest, every single wall had to be stripped of plaster up to shoulder-height from the ground to prepare for the coming of the damp course people. These same thick walls were to be pierced for new windows. The flagged floor of the big old pantry was to be taken up and made damp-proof, and all skirtings and many floorboards and joists were to be riven out and renewed. The builders would be practically living with us, a daunting prospect.

There were strange goings on in the garden that last night. Not for the first time we thanked our lucky stars for the trees that decently screened us from the road and passing motorists.

It had been bad enough getting rid of the chairs and dining tables, entailing as it did a complicated wriggle through two adjacent doorways set at right-angles to each other, with no room to limber up, but the settee almost defeated us. It was long, curved and unyielding and if it hadn't been for the indisputable fact that we had got it *in* there in the first place, we should have given up and let it take its chance among the plaster dust.

Somehow the three of us emerged through the front door. Across the garden and down the bungalow path we marched in slow procession. Gordon was in the lead bearing the Tilley lamp and one end of the settee, and I shuffled after him wearily clinging to the other end. I felt that the best part of my life had been spent treading this pack-horse route to the bungalow. And you know what? The blasted thing wouldn't go through the door.

So there we were — at almost midnight after a typically active day — clearing out the workshop.

There was so much stuff in there that, personally, I shouldn't have voluntarily tackled it in broad daylight with a team of trained Commandos to assist. Hercules, I thought bitterly, didn't know when he was well off.

We picked up the shrouded settee where it waited outside the bungalow door and staggered with it across the garden in the glare of the hissing Tilley, ducking beneath the laden plum branches and chanting the Lyke Wake Dirge as we went.

'This yah neet, this yah neet
Ivery neet an' all
Fire an' fleet an' cannle leet
An' Christ tak up thy soul.'

The ancient dirge sung long ago in these northern hills when it was believed that the souls of the dead passed over Whinny Moor seemed entirely appropriate.

Our next and last burden actually was only a china cabinet, but even in cool, clear daylight Gordon, who had hated it from the moment I had bought it second hand years before, said it was exactly like a glass coffin. I must admit it was, rather. That wouldn't go in the bungalow either so it too was solemnly paraded through the weeping fruit trees and interred in the Stygian darkness of the workshop.

After that we fought our way through the auction room ambience of the bungalow and collapsed into bed.

27 Home and dry

Next morning the builders arrived lock, stock and cement mixer, and were nothing but *nothing* like that earlier pair.

Ted and Andrew were the main theme, as it were, with a handful of others swelling the chord in certain passages, all creating a harmonious whole. Literally as well as figuratively: no transistor toters there. Ted endeared himself to mother from the off, when as he worked, he sang in key the old songs of her youth. The kind with tunes to them. In the dinner hour, if he happened to be there that day, Mr Robinson of the bald head and woolly cap played the piano — peeling back the dustcovers to get to the keys. They were a hard working, friendly crowd and mother and I enjoyed their company. Roger, then aged three, adored them.

Roger spent the whole day, every day, helping them — and they didn't seem to mind a bit. Mixing concrete in the yard with his seaside spade, pushing his little wheelbarrow alongside Andrew's — and Andrew always put a little of whatever he happened to be transporting at the time into it: a dab of concrete, a mound of rubble — and even eating his lunch, especially packed by me for the purpose, with them. And the work progressed efficiently.

While I was shovelling rubble out of the bedroom after the builders had gone for the day, down came Geo Carter to tell me he'd brought the load of straw we'd ordered and he needed Gordon to help him unload it.

When I told him that Gordon wasn't yet home and he'd have to make do with me he wasn't at all pleased. But he wasn't nearly as fed up as I was. I had been hoping that the delivery would be made on Saturday when labour was plentiful, and here it was milking time already and me dying for my tea. I had no choice but to climb up with him to where his lorry was parked by the Browns' house, but I grumbled every inch of the way. I could have saved my breath, he wasn't listening to me. He had a grouse of his own about how he was having to do everything himself since he'd sacked his men that very morning. He was a very powerful, masculine sort of man who, I felt, could take half a dozen men's work in his stride, but when I saw the mountain of straw bales towering heavenwards on top of the waggon and he told me he'd stacked the lot himself, I felt nothing but respectful sympathy. Until he ordered me to get up there on top and start chucking them off.

It was like looking up at the blank face of a warehouse. I could see I should get no gentlemanly helping hand from our Geo who, discounting me entirely, was still moaning about his singlehandedness, so I started scaling various projections on the cab of the lorry which brought me about a sixth of the way up the side of the stack and about a mile off the ground. There I teetered on one foot feeling as useless as Geo Carter thought I was.

I'm not clear about what happened next but I think that Geo got sick of waiting and gave me a shove, because I suddenly shot upwards like a cork from a bottle and landed prone on top of the mountain with a view below on the other side of a passing tractor towing an empty trailer. I just had time to reflect that a *soupçon* more umpty on Geo's part and the trailer would have been full of me, when a stentorian 'Oy!' reminded me that I was not up there to loaf about.

There were millions of bales each weighing upwards of half a ton. Dropping them off was all right — enjoyable even, when I scored a direct hit — but lumping them across from the farther side of the waggon was a bit of a strain. As the stack diminished the new one alongside grew, and I was ordered up on top of *that* to lump the damn things all over again. It was the pace that was so excruciating. Without a break the bales flowed from one stack to the other like sand in an egg timer.

With lacerated hands and profound relief I wrote out the cheque.

'Ta,' said Geo fiercely. 'It's a bloody nuisance me having to do all this on my own.' He slammed into his cab and drove home to his tea.

He was blowed, said Gordon that night as we started to lead the straw down to the farmyard, if he would do it like this next year. He'd have a different arrangement, see if he didn't!

Next day, the scene changed to a flashback of the Wild West.

Dreamily passing the front door on my way to the iris garden I was brought up rigid when two bandits, the lower part of their faces hidden behind triangular scarves, erupted from the house in a cloud of smoke. Curiosity established that the smoke was, in fact, plaster dust. The house was full of it to the degree that it was literally impossible to see half-way across the room. The bandits clawed off their masks and took deep gulps of air, wiping sludge off their faces with equally filthy fore-arms. I felt very sorry for them, but they only laughed and chaffed a bit before rebinding the masks and diving back into the fog.

On the following day the Wild West effect was accentuated with the arrival of the damp course people who added to the atmosphere with sharp reports and flashes of gunpowder as they fused together the copper strips for the damp course, with alarming explosions — oh, the excitement we have at Westwath.

The technicians brought with them a compressor to power the drill used on the outside walls and a generator for the inside ones. What with these pounding and humming, drills screeching through stone, Ted and Co. braying openings for new windows through walls as thick as the length of my arm, and the joiners adding their quota of sawing and hammering, mother and I were glad to go down the garden and pick plums.

Mr Johnson himself was one of the joiners. I happened to be chatting to him as he and his mate prized off the skirting in the living room. To my surprise the reverse of the board was an all over uniform shade of bright yellow.

'That's a funny idea,' I exclaimed in my innocence. 'Painting the *back* of the board.'

Mr Johnson swivelled on his knees and looked at me. 'Paint!' he said, wondering how anyone could be so simple. 'That's not paint. That's dry rot. Look!' He ran a thumb nail beneath the thick yellow skin. 'Fungus, that is. Solid fungus. That,' he went on in case the penny hadn't dropped, 'is the cause of the mushroom smell you've had.'

The builders were with us for more than three weeks and their departure left us feeling almost bereft! We knew they would return after three months — the length of time stipulated by the damp course people between stripping off and replastering the walls — and this time we looked forward to their coming with no qualms whatever. The joiners returned intermittently to complete the renewal of joists and skirtings, spouting and guttering and, joy of joys, to hang a new glass outer door in a flapping, plastic-filled hole in the dining room wall.

Christmas that year was unusual to say the least, with our wall to wall floorboarding and plasterless walls. The castle-like austerity lacked only a noisily fettered ghost or two to complete the picture. The baronial hall effect was heightened by wood fires big enough to roast an ox, burning in every grate. These performed the dual service of destroying the rot-ridden timbers and furthering the house drying out process. The glow from the flames danced on the baubles on the Christmas tree making up for the unavoidable absence of fairy lights, in our electricity-less home. Father Christmas must have been surprised at the hot reception but to everyone's relief he came just as usual.

Roger was taken to his first Carol Service and sang 'Noel, Noel,' to everything regardless and, putting gilt on the gingerbread, Christmas was a white one — just.

True, once the festival was over and the tree and tinsel put away, the castle lost a lot of its glamour and twentieth century sophistication would not have come amiss.

Not that the stripped stone walls were unsightly — far from it. It was the upper half with its century-old plaster reinforced with cow hair and — if the colour was anything to go by and I believe it *was* — another of that animal's products, that got us down. I started surreptitiously stripping it off one of the dining room walls and when the plaster line rose too high to be unremarked — somewhere up near the picture rail — I took a defiant stand and said that was how I wanted it — one wall *au naturel*.

Gordon's restoration project was even more worthwhile. The super carved stone fireplace now stands cleansed of obliterating black lead and paint, and is as the craftsman surely intended it.

In January, to Roger's ecstatic joy, Ted and Andrew returned for two more weeks and with their trowels drew a plaster curtain over the beautifully dressed stone blocks. Except for that one dining room wall which Ted — in whom I had found an ally — pointed up for me.

The farmhouse at Westwath beats with new life, dry and damp proof at last with, thanks to all the new and larger windows, sunshine flooding into corners that had never seen daylight before. All the downstairs rooms are improved — have even swapped identities or gained entirely new ones, a circumstance which adds a little more to our normal confusion — 'Do you mean the *old* kitchen or the *new* one? The back hall or the inner one?'

Of all the improvements the one that delights me most is the creation of the inner hall from the late unlamented dank, dark, windowless pantry. It is lighted now by a new south facing window, furnished with old stripped-wood chests, Aunt Mary's hanging clock and the end wall lined with bookshelves from floor to ceiling. The shelves are full to overflowing and I am pestering Gordon for more.

Just one thing though. It is more than seven years since the builders left us and we haven't yet got round to decorating all the rooms. Things keep cropping up to stop us.

I'll tell you about them someday. When I get rid of these bandages and can hold a pen again.